YOU HAVE
THE POWER

YOU HAVE THE POWER

EXPLORE THE **MINDSET** YOU NEED TO REALISE YOUR DREAMS

PAT FALVEY

Peak Performance & Lifetime Learning Programmes
The Mountain Lodge, Beaufort, Killarney,
County Kerry, Ireland
Tel: 00353 (64) 6644181
Website: www.patfalvey.com
Email: info@patfalvey.com

First published in 2016 by Beyond Endurance Publishing,
Ireland (print and electronic)

ISBN: 978 0 9927125 2 5 (print)
        978 0 9927125 3 2 (ebook)
        978 0 9927125 4 9 (audiobook)

Editorial services by Red Hen Publishing
Typesetting and design by Fairways Design
Printed and bound in the EU

A CIP record for this title is available from the British Library

To all who choose to reach their full potential in life,
following their dreams and goals and making them a reality.

CONTENTS

ACKNOWLEDGEMENTS

Thanks to all the mavericks, leaders, motivators, dreamers, darers and doers who attend my lectures and presentations around the world and who continuously challenge me to move beyond my own comfort zone and explore my full potential.

Thanks to my family who have supported me in all of the challenges I have undertaken during my life and who have always been there for me, keeping the faith in good times and bad.

To my friends and team-mates who have kept me focused and grounded as an individual and who have helped me realise that life is an amazing journey which we honour when we strive to be the best that we can be.

A special thank-you to my editor, Bridget McAuliffe, who was instrumental in ensuring that this book reached the bookshelves. Thanks also to my design and editorial team who quoted my own words to me to ensure we met deadlines. My thanks to the ever-inspiring and insightful Dr John Demartini for writing the foreword to this book.

FOREWORD

Deep inside you is an ageless explorer, an adventurer, an amazing creator capable of creating your inspired and powerful destiny. Though this inner creative giant may have been lying dormant in you now for years, or maybe even your whole lifetime, like a mighty volcano, it stands patiently waiting within, fired up with enthusiasm, ever ready to explode through any of your rigid, cracking and crusty old ways of thinking and feeling to be harnessed for your most powerful purpose and journey. Yes, inside you, you truly have a special gift and creative power waiting to be released.

What if you could liberate this great power lying deep within, have it explode and expand your potential to new heights and create for you a ground-breaking, far-reaching impact on your own life and on the foundational world around you? What if you could perform and achieve at new heights and create a lasting legacy of influence that truly made a meaningful and inspiring difference in the lives of those you love and others?

What if you could master the mindset of great genius, exemplify the heroic role model of inspired leadership and stand on the shoulders of intellectual giants, while not living in the shadows of anyone? Would that not be your true inner aim and ultimate game for a life worth living?

What if you authentically lived by your true highest values and priorities each day and built vast productivity and momentum? What if you held the big picture in view within the executive center of your forebrain as you rose up to greater levels of self-mastery and governance? What if your resultant objective and fearless discipline could break through any obstacles and inspire others to achieve even more as you created your own ever-expanding achievements alongside theirs? What if your degree of grateful love became so transcendent that any transient judgments were melted into a new matrix of more fruitful energies that transformed and served?

What if you were unaffected by the outer praise or criticism of others and remained resilient, centered, committed and focused on your mission each day? What if you were inspired by the invigorating challenges that bring you wellness promoting eustress and were undistracted by any illness resulting distress? What if you dared to dream vastly, congruently and integrally each day as a maverick and masterfully and patiently planned your daily actions and transform apparent obstacles into breathtaking opportunities that other were too frightened to take? What if you objectively preempted and mitigated any illusive risks and so-called potential adversities that could emerge as feedback loops of greater refinement and polish and became an eminent leader along the way?

Could you live an amazing, courageously empowered and adventurous life? Could you allow any momentary limits to be perceived as simply editing symbols for creating an even greater masterpiece that became your refined art of living? Could you enlighten up your load by transcending the superfluous through more efficient and effective achieving? Could your clarity and respectful caring enhance your communication with those who you are intimate with or partners you love and with those who are part of your greater mission and team? Could you be of greater service, surrounded by more abundant resources and receive more expanded economic rewards? The answers to all of these questions are resoundingly yes - once you truly and deeply know that you have the power and diligently explore the mindset required to actualize your dreams.

All of these and even more can and will be yours as you partake of the wisdom gleaned within the pages that follow; pages that are filled with special gems revealed by Pat Falvey as he shares his own self-mastering and mindful journey with the power. If you are ready to begin celebrating with humble gratitude your future series of amazing achievements then begin now devouring the mentoring words that follow in these insightful pages and come to know what your innermost being has always known that *You Have the Power* to create your dreams.

DR JOHN DEMARTINI – International best-selling author of *The Values Factor – The Secret to Creating an Inspired and Fulfilling Life*

INTRODUCTION

For much of my life I have been an explorer, adventurer and entrepreneur. I have travelled to the furthest regions of planet Earth and have had the honour of being in places that few others get to go to, seeing nature in all its pristine majesty and ferocity. For over 30 years, I have worked with and helped thousands of people to follow their dreams with conviction and passion to make their goals reality. Personally, I have had spectacular successes and failures in my life and have learned many lessons along the way.

The most profound thing I have learned is that the greatest exploration of all is the exploration of our mindset. What goes on in our mind colours our days and shapes our life. We are what we think and how we think; therefore it is vitally important that we explore our mindset to see if it is our friend or enemy in life, helping us or preventing us from leading the life we want to lead. I have also learned that each and every one of us is ordinary and that it is what we do, think and act on that makes our life extraordinary.

My own life has been a roller coaster. I was born into a family of bricklayers in a close-knit working-class community on the north side of Cork city in Ireland. I, too, was destined to become a bricklayer. But my grandmother and earliest mentor, Mary B., taught me when I was a child that I could be and do anything I wanted. I went to live with her when I was six years old and became her apprentice. By the time I was ten years of age, I had my first business, collecting second-hand clothes that Mary B. would later sell at local markets.

With the self-belief she instilled in me, I left school at 15 years of age to become a millionaire. I started work as a bricklayer but soon moved into property development. I was young, hungry, full of energy and believed that the world was mine for the taking. By the time I was 23, I had achieved my goals. I was living in my dream house, owned flashy cars and was married with two young children. I worked hard, played hard and was ruthless. I was making more money than I believed was possible and loving every minute of it.

But life had hard lessons in store for me. The recession of the 1980s exposed all my weaknesses—I wasn't looking at the bigger picture and didn't see the downturn coming. I took my eye off the ball and lost my business due to overtrading, selfishness and greed. My self-esteem and confidence were at an all-time low. I became depressed and tried to take my own life through suicide on 6 September 1986 when I drove towards an open wharf at high speed. Moments from entering the water, an image of my young sons' faces appeared before me. I slammed on the brakes and the car stopped just before it would have entered the river. I was totally shaken and wept at the quayside.

I had no other dream, no other plan. I, who had believed that I was invincible, was failing; I felt trapped and ashamed. I could no longer cope, but 1980s Ireland wasn't a place where anyone, especially a man, could admit that. However, the people around me knew the situation I was in and, while no one addressed my emotional distress openly, they did what they could to help.

One day, my secretary's father, an avid hillwalker, came to my office and insisted that I join his group the following Sunday for a hike. I had zero interest or energy for such activity but he wouldn't go away and I agreed just to get rid of him. He still didn't go away and on a Sunday when I felt I should be in my office worrying about everything, I found myself with a group of strangers heading for the mountains of Kerry.

That first climb changed my life. I was way out of my comfort zone. I had to focus on each step I took and my natural instinct to succeed kicked in; I was determined to get to the mountain top. When I got there I felt something I hadn't felt in a long time: I had succeeded at something. I liked that feeling and wanted it again. I went back to Cork energised by my first ever climb and looking forward to the next one. All that week, I was buzzing with new energy. I was viewing my problems differently, more positively, although I didn't know why.

The next week, I climbed Carrauntuohil, Ireland's highest mountain. I felt alive again. That Sunday, I told my fellows climbers I was going to climb Mount Everest, the world's highest mountain. They thought I was mad. I didn't care; I was going to do it. Seven years later I stood on the summit of Everest for the first time. After that, I became an explorer, visiting some of the most beautiful, remote and hostile parts of the planet. I climbed Everest four times, summiting twice. I jointly led the first Irish team to reach the South Pole, led the first Irish crossing of Greenland, while also leading teams and succeeding in over 80 other exciting adventures throughout the world.

In my adventures, I met people from almost every country in the world and learned that more unites us than divides us. I returned to business life, older and wiser, bringing with me the lessons I had learned from my first big failure, and all that I had learned while I travelled around the world, challenging myself to the limits of my capabilities and exploring who I really was.

During those years I learned valuable lessons that have become my guiding principles in life. The most important truth I learned is that life is an adventure and the greatest exploration of all is how we engage with our mindset so that we can live our best life. In *You Have The Power*, I outline the lessons I have learned throughout my business and adventure life, the insights I have gained from the many people I have encountered, people who take up the challenge that life is to be lived and who set out on that journey, no matter what age they are, how much money they have, or what education or job they have.

In *You Have The Power* you will learn how to become an explorer in the journey of your own life; how to create a legacy that you will be proud of; how to manage your mindset so that it is your friend and ally; how to break free from that idea that there is only one version of yourself that you can be. The book takes a realistic and constructive approach to dealing with the mindset challenges we all face on a daily basis. You will learn how to deal with habitual procrastination, unfounded fears, prejudice, criticism and stress. A big problem facing many of us is that we don't know what we want; we don't allow ourselves freedom to dream and don't know the tools that we need to be able to dream in full colour. I learned early in life that we should dream big, that we should visualise our dreams as if they were already reality, then fuel our want with passion, ambition and self-belief.

Once we identify what we want, then we must take action. Without action, nothing happens but many of us stop at this juncture between dreaming and acting. You must make a decision about what you want, formulate a goal, make a plan, set a time-frame. I analyse the attributes needed to make goals, which include commitment, focus, patience, sacrifice and courage.

My years in formal education were not successful and the greatest knowledge I gained in my life was outside the school walls. The countries I travelled to and the people I met have made me a lifelong student. As such, I am always on a learning continuum, from apprentice to master, forever learning and teaching. I detail how you can really engage with the adventure of your life by becoming open to learning new skills, getting out of your comfort zone, challenging yourself, making mistakes, getting to know your limits and moving beyond them.

As an adventurer, my mind and my body were the main 'engines' I had to get me to the upper reaches of high-altitude mountains and to the furthest points of the Poles. There was no back-up and no opportunity to take it easy. I learned that we have to look after our mind and body throughout life if we want to give ourself the best chance to succeed. We need to be clear on what we stand for, we need to develop healthy networks and we need to feed both our body and mind healthy 'food', whether in the form of actual food or in the form of the self-talk that is ongoing in our head.

Throughout life, becoming and remaining efficient helps us achieve our goals. To do this, we need to look at the rules we are living by and ask if they are serving or limiting us. We need to learn how to travel light, both in our physical and our mental life. Baggage of all sorts weighs us down and impedes progress. In *You Have The Power* you will learn how to identify what you need to keep, and what you need to discard. Clear communication is a key attribute of efficiency and one around which we can't afford to make assumptions. Check and re-check that what you are saying is being heard and that what you are hearing is what is being said.

Life is full of challenge and there are clear lessons to be learned on how to successfully negotiate challenge. This book teaches you how to deal with risk, danger, crisis, conflict and adversity. How we approach challenges and opportunities shapes our experience of life. Consequently, we need to learn about the importance of attitude and the choices we have when it comes to how we face each day. I have learned that choosing to be happy, grateful, humble and caring makes life easier, while laughter and celebration are as important as the air that we breathe.

One of the biggest challenges facing all of us today is finding balance in a world where choice is unlimited. Too much choice often makes us want to give up before we even start but we can all learn ways to achieve a good work-life balance and to have a balanced approach to money so that it serves us and our communities. Underpinning all of this is the need to have a strong balance between the emotional and logical parts of our mind.

I outline what I call the 'inevitabilities' of life and how best to deal with them—making and breaking habits; the dangers of complacency; obsession; the value of failing; defining success; changing course when it's necessary; dealing with defeat; challenging yourself to be the best that you can be at any given time.

As long as we live, we will be dealing with people and learning how to work well with others—from family members to colleagues and strangers—is one of the most valuable lessons in life. We want to make our relationships work. I learned on expedition—where a breakdown in relations between team members was potentially fatal—the vital nature of effective teamwork. I outline lessons in becoming an effective team player, self-leader, leader and mentor. I also share the lessons I have learned about the values and pitfalls of partnerships and collaborations.

As we cross the finish line when our goal is finally reached, we should always know what's next. The adventure of life is ongoing and we are always capable of achieving something more that will bring us closer to being the people we are capable of becoming.

No matter what we have done or not done up to this point, what is important is how we live the life we have left. Be open to possibility and opportunity. Look at the bigger picture. View your life as a journey of adventure and self-discovery. Be curious about the world. Have courage. Learn, as the Irish poet John O'Donohue writes, to *find ease in risk*. Look for the joy in every challenge, no matter how difficult. Dream big and remember that it is in the following of the dream that the success lies; achieving your goal is a bonus.

EXPLORE THE LIMITS OF WHO YOU CAN BE

We are explorers on the greatest expedition of all—the physical, mental, emotional and spiritual journey that is human life. This life we have been given is a gift and it is important that we engage with it—no matter what age we are, what we are doing or how we feel—to ensure that while we live we are awake to our journey and our role as co-author of our own destiny.

Too often we forget this: we forget that we are on a journey, that we have a specific—though unknown—amount of time allocated for that journey; we forget that we are moving forward every single day and that we will never re-live any moment of our life; we forget that every moment matters and that we must become conscious of that fact. Let's remember that, no matter where we are in life, now is the best time to actively engage with the exploration of our life and become the author of our own life story.

I

Become an explorer in the journey of your own life

Life isn't a rehearsal, it's a performance

Age is no barrier to new beginnings

Create a legacy you can be proud of

Your life is important; live it to the best of your ability

\# Become an explorer in the journey of your own life

I am the master of my fate:
I am the captain of my soul.

William Ernest Henley

From the minute we are born to the minute we die, we are on a journey. Each life has the exact same beginning and end: birth and death. These events are universal to every human being. What happens in between makes up each individual, unique life. Birth happens to us. Death happens to us. What about the time in-between—our lifetime? Does that also 'happen' to us? Age-old discussion on this subject argues both sides. On the one hand, it is said that we are controlled by a divine force that doesn't allow self-determination; on the other, it is argued that we are entirely self-determining and have full responsibility for our life.

The truth, as always, is somewhere in-between. We are given the gift of human life. We don't know when we will enter or exit this world and there is a whole range of aspects of our life over which we have no control. We can, however, control how we experience the life that we have been gifted. We can decide our reaction to each and every experience. We can, in fact, shape our life by both our anticipation of and reaction to what each day brings. The poet Seamus Heaney wrote, 'The way we are living, timorous or bold, will have been our life'. Life is an amazing journey of adventure and we have a choice to make—we can stay in the valley and gaze at those who are on their way to their summit, or we can climb the mountain peaks we want to achieve.

No matter who we are, we all have our own private Everest to scale. Getting to the summit is not always guaranteed and it's hard work. It requires want, commitment, focus, hunger and passion to reach our objectives. These are key ingredients for achieving our full potential and for realising our goals in all areas of life—family, home, work, wealth, love and contentment.

Life is an amazing adventure

I believe we should all engage with the journey of our life as if it was the most important and exciting adventure that we could ever go on.

We should dream about the adventures—big and small—that make up the journey of our life. We must make plans and act on those plans so that we give ourself the best possible chance of reaching our goals every time we set them.

Too often, we don't dream, we don't plan and we don't act. We expect things to happen, to be given to us; we become complacent and lazy. We neither set nor achieve goals and then we begin to regret the things we haven't done, the time we have wasted, the skills we didn't tap into, the opportunities we didn't explore. It is, however, never too

> ## We are the architects of our own life

late to engage with the adventure of life, no matter what age we are. Wherever we are in life is a perfect starting point for a new dream and a new goal. The challenge to live fully is there even if we don't take it up; it is always waiting for us.

We are the architects, the engineers and the builders in our own life. As such, we must ensure that we have the design and plan in place before we start building what we desire. Like a building, our life will need repairs and maintenance to keep it in good condition. This is why we should do a regular life audit. This will help us to be sharper, to be self-aware, to be well-informed and able to change direction when change is required. Too many of us never take the time to check in with where we are at. Then we become resentful when we believe that we have left it too late to have the life we want.

Ask yourself:

- How are you living your life? Are you content? Frustrated? Happy?

- Are you timorous or bold in your engagement with your life and your potential?

- Are you open to opportunity when it arises in the journey of your life?

- Do you meet each day filled with hope and self-belief or apathy and self-doubt?

● Are you living a full life or enduring what feels like a half-life in the hope that tomorrow, next week, next month or next year will bring something better?

Each day is precious; it may or may not be our last day, but what is for sure is that it is a period of time that we will never live again. We cannot stop time and no moment should be a rehearsal for a better one; there is only now. When we view life as a journey, then each day brings a new part of the road to be travelled.

● Do you know where you will be at the end of this day?

● How far will you have travelled?

● How will you experience and react to the happenings of the day?

● How will what you go through today shape your anticipation of tomorrow?

We have a lot more control over how we live our todays and tomorrows than we might even want to acknowledge. It is so much easier to make excuses for why our life isn't the one we thought we would be living, the one we feel we deserve, the one we will be living once X and Y and Z happen. It takes a lot more courage and hard work—both mental and physical—to look at ourself and our life honestly and unemotionally and say, 'No more excuses, from this moment on I will be an active agent in my own life'.

By having the courage to take action, to own our own power, to be the architect of our own life, we consciously engage with the challenge of discovering what we are capable of doing, achieving and becoming. Our life then becomes an adventure of self-discovery, of learning, of failing, of succeeding, of achieving, of full living. We should all be active agents in our own life. We need to take responsibility for how we are living our life and, more importantly, how we react to our life. We are capable of so much more than we realise. We need to have dreams and goals and the belief that we can achieve what we want in life. Then, when we take our first steps, we will gain the confidence of experience.

Each life offers a unique opportunity for exploring the world from a new perspective: our own. We learn about the world and life from the stories of others but we also need to create our own stories, based on our own experiences of life, the world and its people. The more we explore and the more adventures we undertake, the more stories we create that become the raw material of our unique experience. We learn about who we are and who we can become. We become explorers of our unique potential and learn to push the boundaries of what we believe we are capable of learning, dreaming, daring, doing and achieving.

> **Learn to push the boundaries of what you believe you are capable of**

By having exciting goals and aspirations, by having detailed plans, by having a positive mindset and self-belief, by accepting that we have to engage with risk to move forward, each one of us can set out on a life journey of adventure, exploration and learning, of constant challenge, failure and achievement.

Life isn't a rehearsal, it's a performance

From the time we are born, we are dying. On a planet that is 4.4 billion years old, the average human life expectancy in the Western world is 80 years while in some Third World countries it is as low as 40 years. In the vastness of the cosmos, we are a mere blip in time. Yet, the very fact of being alive is a gift and we should grasp every opportunity to live to the fullest expression of our personal potential during our allocated time on Earth.

The time we are given to live is priceless, it is our greatest asset and it is free. But we take it mostly for granted and don't value it as we should. We cannot buy time; we cannot extend it, trade it or sell it. Time is ours to use in whatever way we want. We can waste it or we can use it to create our dream life, to achieve our personal bucket list, to develop our potential and create a great legacy.

Not one of us knows how long we will live. We all know people who have died prematurely—children, students, young adults and friends that died far too soon. This knowledge should serve as a timely reminder to honour every year, month, week, day and minute of our existence. We should celebrate our life by making the most of the gift we have been given; by being the best that we can be; by living interesting, valuable lives and by leaving behind the best possible legacy that we can.

- 80 years = 960 months = 4,160 weeks = 29,200 days

- Assess where you are in terms of the average lifespan

- Are you happy with how you are living your life right now?

- If not, now is the moment to make the decision to start living the life that you want

Once, during an interview on national radio, the presenter asked me if I thought that adventurers are selfish because, by following our dreams of travelling to the most dangerous parts of the planet, there is an increased risk that we will die. A friend and fellow explorer had recently died while on expedition in Antarctica and the presenter wondered why people travelled to places where the risk of dying was so high. I explained that I have completed numerous expeditions to some of the harshest environments in the world and survived. I've had wonderful experiences during my travels, learning about different cultures and experiencing life among many

> Honour the gift of your life

different native tribes. As well as experiencing the thrill of being where few people have the opportunity to travel, this life is my passion. My family, I said, have always been very supportive of my passion and are very proud of my achievements. To honour the trust they have in me, I have always been meticulous in my planning, ensuring that all risk is minimised. But there will always be some degree of risk, not alone in the life of adventurers but in all of our lives, no matter who we are or what we do.

I went on to explain that, in October 2015, I attended hospital for a routine check-up and, within 24 hours, due to a complication with the procedure, I developed sepsis and was only hours from total organ failure but, thankfully, made a full recovery. Three months later, a friend went into hospital with tendonitis. He, too, developed sepsis but didn't survive and died at the age of 56. These experiences reinforced my long-held

Never put off what you want to do in life

belief that we should never put off what we want to do in life. We do not know how much time we have left and it makes sense to live every moment as if it were our last.

Sometimes we wrap ourself protectively in cotton wool, afraid to challenge ourself, to step outside the box and to live the life that, deep down, we want to live. We owe it to ourself to make the most of our life while we are on Earth. Too many of us don't do this. We don't fulfil our dreams, goals or aspirations because of fear—fear of critics, fear of failure, fear of ridicule, fear of success, fear of the demands that following our dreams or fulfilling our goals requires, fear of change. It is often very hard to find the courage needed to step out of the comfort zone of the habitual and into the journey of adventure that our life should be; the journey that allows us to reach our full potential.

We all need to be active agents in our own life and to take responsibility for how we are living that life. An effective way to do this is to make the fact of our death a constant companion. The Irish poet John O'Donohue wrote, 'From the moment you were born, your death has walked beside you'. Its presence acts as a reminder to live life intensely and joyfully, squeezing as much as possible out of each day.

When we accept the inevitability of death, it brings peace of mind and acts as a wake-up call to live the best life that

Challenge your limits

we are capable of living, the life that we would love to look back on from our deathbed when the end comes. No matter what age we are, what skills we have, what educational qualifications we have, what job we are in or what baggage we are carrying, now is the right time to explore the possibilities of our life. Now is the time to achieve something we have always wanted to achieve, to fulfil a dream and challenge the limits of our capabilities.

We should regularly ask ourself: 'If I were to die today, would I leave this world having lived the life that I wanted to live?' If the answer is no, then we need to do something about it. We need to see what we can change and make those changes. One of the most valuable lessons I ever learned was from the Buddhist monks in Tengboche monastery high in the Himalaya. Life, they say, isn't a rehearsal, it's a performance.

● Live your life as if it was your most important performance ever

● Fear only the regret of not having followed your dreams

Age is no barrier to new beginnings

The secret of genius is to carry the spirit of the child into old age, which means never losing your enthusiasm.

Aldous Huxley

We are never too old or too young to make radical changes and start anew. Adventure is not the preserve of those under an arbitrarily chosen age. All around the world, people are defying what society tells them is age-appropriate and embracing the adventure of life as they explore the limits of what they can do at their current age.

In 1991, when I was 34, I was walking to Everest Base Camp when I saw a man coming towards me. I was taken aback when I saw him; he appeared to be very old and I wondered how he had found his way to that remote area. I was curious and asked him what he was doing. He said that his name was John and that his dream was to go to Everest Base Camp. He was 85 years old. I was stunned and wanted to know more about him. We retired to a local tea house where he introduced me to Jean, his 79-year-old partner. John told me that they were planning to go to Antarctica to celebrate his 90th birthday. When they spoke, I felt as if I was talking to people in their twenties.

This couple became an inspiration to me and, years later, when I was in my fifties, I set up the Forever Young Club, for 50- to 90-year-olds who are seeking new challenges. Meeting John and Jean gave me a valuable perspective on life and ageing which acts as a positive influence on my own life and those of the people I work with, right up to the present day. I look forward to being 85 as I know I will still be part of a community of adventurers who believe that age is no barrier to living a full life.

Throughout our life, we should continue to set new goals and to scale them to where we are in our life journey. We can always do much more than we imagine; the thing is to remember this and to keep exploring, to keep pushing until we reach our limit for today, and not let people tell us we are too young or too old to live the life we want.

- There are always new adventures awaiting you no matter what age you are

- Accept that ageing is part of the process of life

- Accept that there will always be things you must give up, and new things you can learn

Create a legacy you can be proud of

No matter who we are or what we do—be that a parent, teacher, leader, politician, company CEO, a team or an organisation—we all want to leave a legacy that we can be proud of. As we go through life and accumulate stuff, we think of the material legacy that we will leave to our family and friends—our homes, money, valuables, and individual items that mean so much to us. We think long and hard about what will mean most to whom; who deserves what; who we want to surprise with an unexpected gift.

We should spend as much time thinking about the legacy of ourself—stripped of the material items we accumulate during our life—and how we are in the world. If we think about the legacy of our presence, it really helps us focus on how we are turning up right now, today, in our own life, for ourself and for those we encounter. How do our actions, behaviour and contributions affect those around us? How do they affect our family, friends, teams, companies and wider society?

> Every life has a purpose

Every single life has a purpose and when we think consciously about our legacy, we start to focus on the decisions we are making every day about how we live. By being conscious of our legacy, we can aim to lead a more creative and worthwhile life, not just as individuals but also as organisations, companies or governments.

If we think about the legacy we have created up to this point in time, how would we describe it? The main legacy that I have created is one where I have been blessed to have the opportunity to inspire people to challenge themselves and to introduce thousands of people to the life-enhancing and healing joy of the great outdoors. I have encouraged young people with disabilities to hike and climb in the hills, and worked with many charities whose existence helps ease the burdens that people have to carry in life.

Consider your legacy at this precise moment:

- How would you describe yourself?

- How would your family and friends describe you?

- What have you done that has brought you most joy?

- Is there anything you regret not doing?

- What are your dreams?

- Have you followed them? If not, why?

- Are you satisfied with the life you have led up to this point?

- Have you made the most of your skills and of the opportunities that came your way?

- Who have you spent your time with and what kind of impact have they had on your life?

- What do you stand for in life?

- How engaged have you been with family, friends, colleagues and community?

No matter what we have done—or not done—up to this point, what is important is how we live our life from this moment forward. We need to use the knowledge that we won't live forever as a tool that sharpens our determination to live the best life that we can, to follow and fulfil our dreams and to create the legacy that we want to leave behind.

From this moment:

- Start living the life that you are capable of living

- Start exploring the extent of your capabilities in the knowledge that you are far more capable than you ever before thought possible

- Know that no matter what age you are, what skills you have, what educational qualifications you have, what job you are in, or what emotional baggage you are carrying, you still have the opportunity to dream and achieve

We are the lucky ones to be in a position to ponder this issue. We should honour our good fortune by ensuring that our legacy is something we consciously engage with. We shape it and it, in turn, shapes our life. We don't have to be famous (or infamous) or of worldwide renown to leave a legacy; we all have the power of one and each one of us contributes, in one way or another, to shaping the world.

Your life is important; live it to the best of your ability

Act as if what you do makes a difference. It does.

William James

Every person is important. Each one of us makes a difference during our life and we all impact in some way on the world during our time in it. It is not necessarily the person who is making the most noise or the most money or surrounded by the most people who is having the most profound impact. We all leave our footprint on the Earth. It is not enough, however, for us to accept the fact that our existence matters; we need to have it recognised. In short, we need to feel that we are important—to those closest to us, to our community and within our workplace. When we feel important, our self-belief increases, as does our ability to believe in others and in our collective potential.

Why do we want to feel important to other people? Why isn't it enough to go through life doing our best and hoping to leave a worthwhile legacy? Why do we need regular confirmation of our worth from others? Life would be so much easier if we didn't need to be acknowledged, but it is a basic human need to feel important, to be loved, to have our presence and our contribution marked by others. We often feel guilty about this need and some of us go to great lengths to deny this basic desire. We can become so self-effacing that, ironically, those around us are at pains to make us feel important.

Recognise your own importance

Many of us find it very hard to accept compliments. When my first book was published, I was overwhelmed by the number of people who requested that I sign it for them. I constantly shied away from the prospect because I did not feel worthy of their recognition even though, deep down, I wanted to accept their request and feel proud of my achievement. Then, one day, a friend pulled me aside and said: 'Pat, do you know that you are being insulting by hiding away from these people's compliments?' He explained that I was making people uncomfortable by my rebuffs and he advised that I should accept the intended honour and say, 'Thank you for the compliment'. I started to do that and it made such a difference. It boosted my self-esteem and I stopped making those around me feel uncomfortable when wishing me well.

- Accept compliments gracefully and give thanks to those who admire you

- When you accept compliments with sincere gratitude, you feel stronger and more confident

It is much healthier and less time-consuming if we just acknowledge our need to feel important, which is consistent with our need to be loved, wanted and needed. This need comes from our very core as human beings. We tell young children they are most important people in the world. Someone probably said this to most of us when we were very young and it gave us a sense of being wanted, being honoured and being important; in short, of mattering. As we grow into adulthood, it is assumed—and we also assume—that we no longer need these assurances. But we do, whether we like it or not.

Strange as it may seem, it is often very small things that make us feel like we matter and that our contribution is appreciated. A factory manager I know needed to get reports on a monthly basis from workers coming off the night shift. The workers were tired, resistant and non-compliant when it came to giving the necessary details after their night's work. The new manager recognised how they were feeling and arranged to have good quality refreshments given to them when they came off their shift.

Accept compliments with gratitude

The workers reacted positively and were happy to give all details to the manager. What had changed? The new manager had recognised the workers' importance. She had acknowledged how they were feeling after a long night's shift. She respected them and the role they were playing within the organisation. And all it took was some hot tea and decent biscuits, but the gesture was sincerely meant.

When we feel unimportant, our self-belief and our confidence in our own ability are undermined. We can feel that what we are doing is undervalued or even without value. When we take others for granted, we diminish their sense of the value

You are alive; you matter

of their contribution, and the same happens us when our contribution goes unappreciated. People talk of becoming invisible, especially as they grow older in a world that idolises youth. This 'invisibility' comes from a sense of no longer mattering in the world; what we say or do seems of no consequence. This treatment of each other is damaging, not only to those who we think no longer matter or have little left to contribute, but also to ourself. Unless we stop, it is us that will be in that position when we become 'invisible'.

When elderly people do wild things, the world sits up and takes notice. Why? Because they are doing the unexpected; they are saying, 'I am important. I still matter. I am still alive'. We like it because we hope they shine a light on our future that shows we are important no matter what age we are. Accepting that we are important, that everyone else is important, that we all make a contribution that has value and that we need to get and give recognition for those contributions is a simple, yet vital, lesson in gaining a healthy mindset for our life journey. Once learned, it engenders respect and gratitude for ourself and for others.

I have the power to:

- Dream and set goals

- Be courageous

- Take action

- Achieve my full potential

- Conquer my fears and take action

- Live my best life

MANAGE YOUR MINDSET TO SUCCEED

Our mindset—what goes on in our mind and the ongoing conversation we have with ourself—is one of the most powerful factors shaping how we live our life. To gain control over how we engage with and react to the events and experiences that constitute our life, we must engage with our mindset, examine our self-talk and analyse the factors that influence it. These factors include our family history and ancestry, along with the history, expectations and limitations of our community and wider society.

These inherited stories create our foundations and shape not only the life we live, but also who we believe we are and can be. We should constantly examine our identity 'inheritance' to see if it is serving us or imprisoning us. By revisiting our inherited story, we can discover how it shapes us and how, in turn, we can re-interpret it so that it doesn't limit who we are and who we can become.

2

Manage your mindset so that is it your friend and not your enemy

Build strong foundations throughout your life

Identify your role models: cherish the good ones and move away from the bad ones

Use your heroes to inspire you to action

Shared stories help make sense of who you are and who you can become

Who you are today is but one manifestation of who you are capable of being

Always remember there is a bigger picture

Manage your mindset so that it is your friend and not your enemy

We are shaped by our thoughts; we become what we think. When the mind is pure, joy follows like a shadow that never leaves.

Buddha

Our mindset is vitally important because, essentially, it determines how we live our life. Mindset can be defined as the habitual attitude or mental approach that shapes how we perceive and respond to life experiences and situations. An open mindset is one that is set for growth, that is open to opportunity, that embraces adventure, that is curious about the world and the people in it, that believes in our ability to achieve. Above all, an open mindset is one that is not ruled by fear. A closed mindset, on the other hand, is ruled by fear and doubt. It is not open to adventure, to learning, or to other ways of being in the world.

To fully engage with our life journey and experience it in all its fullness, we need to have an open mindset. If we don't already have one, we can use some simple tools and actions to acquire a mindset that allows us experience life in a more positive manner. The first issue to examine when it comes to managing our mindset is the importance of negative and positive responses to life. Studies show that the human brain is biased negative for a very valid reason—so that we are alert to danger and can ready ourself before it arrives. This bias has been developing since hunter-gatherer times and has proved vital for ensuring survival in times of threat. Consequently, we tend to consider negative events to have a greater importance than positive ones, which is very helpful when our health or life is endangered.

> An open mindset is not ruled by fear

The result of this naturally negative bias, however, is that we have to develop skills and habits to counter our instinctive reaction to back away from change. We have to consciously work on having a positive reaction and outlook, especially when there is no real threat or danger present. These negative-countering skills are simple and effective when practised over a period of time.

- Use positive self-talk where you tell yourself the positive version of the story that is currently in your head

- Affirm your belief in your ability to deal with whatever you are undertaking

- Use an honest question-and-answer session: What is the worst thing that can happen? What will you do if it does happen? How likely it is to happen in reality?

- Laugh, even when you don't feel like it. Fake laughter works too as the brain doesn't know the difference between fake and real laughter and will respond to both, releasing endorphins which are good for overall emotional wellbeing

- Keep the bigger picture in mind

We should move away, mentally and physically, from negative thoughts and experiences. We should literally get up and walk away into another room, start another conversation or become engaged elsewhere. We must continue the conversation with both the negative and positive brain, working always to balance the inherent negative bias with positivity. Then we can seek and maintain a positive focus and act on the positive messages we are sending to the brain. In this way, we train the brain towards the positive.

We can also develop a personal mantra that helps bring the mind to a place where it is calm. This may be a word or a series of words that don't need to have meaning for anyone else but whose repetition helps focus our mind when it starts wandering all over the place. I

Get your own mantra and repeat it often

always think of my grandmother and the mantra she ingrained in my mind when I was a young boy: 'If you think you can you will and if you think you can't you won't.' I repeat these words to remind myself that my mindset is constantly shaping my life.

We need to learn to recognise when a negative response is the wrong one. If, for example, we are about to undertake something that we are well able to do and a voice in our head starts telling us that we can't do it, and that, even if we could, there is no point, then we must counter that negativity with positive self-talk. We should not allow the negative eat away at our motivation to succeed.

We still need to use the negative bias when we are threatened or in danger because it keeps us alert and focused; it also helps us avoid unrealistic optimism which can prevent us from making realistic assessments and blind us to the need for proper preparation, learning and planning. It is all about challenging ourself and reaching a balanced position, based on measured risk assessment. As we become aware of and work on our mindset, we also become aware of the mindset of the people around us.

Ask the following questions:

- Is their mindset open or closed?

- Are they habitually negative or positive?

- How does their mindset and the energy they radiate impact on you?

- Do you agree with others even if you don't really believe what they are saying to be true, just for the sake of belonging to the group and out of a sense of loyalty to those within it?

A very common example of this can frequently be seen during tea breaks in workplaces, where one person starts complaining about the boss and everyone else agrees because it's more important to be part of the peer group than to question the validity of what is being said. For many of us, complaining is habitual; we are not seeking any resolution and, in fact, may not want one. But this habit of negativity is detrimental and limits any possibility of resolution. A negative mindset will always find reasons why something cannot—or should not—happen.

The negative mindset says:

- It's too hard

- I'll probably fail

- It's not worth the effort

Our negative mindset talk is coming from a place of fear of challenge and fear of moving beyond our comfort zone. With a positive mindset, we perceive the exact same challenges as opportunities.

The positive mindset says:

- This is a fantastic opportunity

- It's worth the effort

- I might succeed and, if I do, I will be so much closer to living the life that I want

- It'll be fun to try

- I'll learn something along the way even if I don't succeed

- Doing something beats doing nothing

Awareness of what feeds our mindset is as important as awareness of what feeds our physical body. We try to feed our body with healthy food and, similarly, we need to feed our mind with healthy thoughts. We have to be strong enough to eradicate negative influences from our life, as they can destroy our creativity, our achievements and our enjoyment of living. We should spend time with positive people, doing things that uplift us, especially when we are finding it hard to maintain the balance between negative and

Stop habitual complaining

positive. We may, in fact, need to avoid certain people for a while so that we can train ourself to access positive bias.

An open mindset with a positive bias allows us expand our expectations of ourself and our life. We will not only believe that we are capable of more, we will actually become capable of more because we are open to trying and achieving.

- Strive for an open mindset

- Observe the people in your life and how their mindset impacts on yours

- Engage in a conversation between the negative and positive response mechanism in your brain

- Practise positive thinking

- Believe in yourself

Build strong foundations throughout your life

If we are lucky, we get our first solid foundations in life from a loving, stable family that is secure in itself, part of a community and focused in its beliefs. We really are blessed if we get such a strong start from which to build and develop our own life. Nonetheless, whatever our original foundations, throughout our life we need to check repeatedly to see if they are strong enough for what lies ahead. We would not build a skyscraper on the foundation for a one-storey house or the building will collapse.

Life is ever-changing and we should check our foundations regularly to see if they can support our dreams and plans and the challenges that we will face in the future. If they aren't strong enough, then we need to invest time and energy in underpinning the ones we have or constructing new ones.

To have strong foundations in life:

- Know yourself

- Love yourself

- Have a clear belief system

- Develop and sustain loyal ties with family and friends

- Create a strong and clearly identified support network

- Ensure you have proper training and skills

- Have good discipline

- Have a good work ethic

- Be compassionate

- Have worthwhile goals

Without strong foundations, our journey will be much harder and reaching our goals less likely. Foundations not only provide the strong base on which we stand, they also provide the strength from which we draw, especially in times of challenge. If they can't sustain us, chances are that what we are building and achieving will feel as if it is on very shaky ground. If we imagine our foundations as roots of a tree going deep into sustaining soil and our life journey as the branches that grow from that tree, we see that the deeper the roots, the stronger and healthier the branches.

Develop strong foundations on which to build your life

Strong foundations offer us the chance to expand in many directions while also allowing us return to our deep-rooted system from which to draw nourishment to continue to grow and expand.

Identify your role models: cherish the good ones and move away from the bad ones

From the moment we are born, we are being shaped and moulded by role models. In our earliest years especially, we may not even be aware that the people around us have such an enormous effect on shaping how we think and who we become as they pass on their value and belief systems to us. Parents, grandparents, older siblings and members of our community all play a role in shaping the young people in their lives. As adults, we should recognise that we are all role models for those around us. We don't always recognise the effects of our behaviour which is why we often see behaviours passed down from generation to generation.

As we grow older, we start to choose our role models, people who, for whatever reason, we admire and look up to and aspire to being like. Role models act as a light, illuminating the way ahead. Without role models, it is often so much harder to find our way. I think of role models as trail breakers who have done the hard work and carved the path ahead of us, making us want to follow in their footsteps.

> **Role models act as a light to show the way**

One of my earliest role models was Mary B., my grandmother, who taught me confidence and positivity, especially when facing challenge and adversity. She instilled in me the belief that I could be anything I wanted to be; that, if I chose, I could challenge the assumption that I would carry on the family tradition of being a bricklayer. When I was six years old, I went to live with Mary B. who could neither read nor write. After school and at weekends, I worked as an apprentice carter with her. Pushing an old pram that she'd bought for me, I went from house to house collecting second-hand clothes. Mary B. would then sell those clothes at markets in the city and around the county. She paid me for my work and, by the time I was ten years old, I had £1,000 in the bank and was the richest child in our working-class community.

One day, when I was delivering clothes to her stall in the city, I was stopped by some American tourists who wanted to take a photograph of me. I agreed, but asked for—and got—payment for posing for them.

I heard them say that Irish people were happy in their poverty and that we were better off that way. Later, at home, I told Mary B. about my day. She became angry when I told her what the tourists had said. I didn't really understand why but I've never forgotten her reaction.

Seek out good role models throughout your life

She pulled me by the ear and stood me in front of three pictures hanging on her kitchen wall. The pictures, which meant the world to her, were of the Sacred Heart, the president of Ireland, Éamon de Valera, and the American president, John F. Kennedy. She told me to look at Kennedy, a man she regarded highly. 'Do you see that man?' she said. 'He is the most powerful person in the world and you are as important and as intelligent as he is and don't let anyone tell you anything different.' I was inspired by her belief in me and by the time I left school at the age of 15, my ambition was to become a millionaire, an ambition I realised, powered by the influence and training of Mary B., my first and most influential role model.

There are always role models in our life. We should ensure that we keep the good ones and move away from those whose direction does not serve us. All our role models are human and we should remember that they, too, are limited and shaped by their life circumstances and are also capable of making mistakes.

- Seek positive role models

- Get rid of bad role models

- Be aware of the fact that you, too, are a role model, especially to family, work colleagues and younger people in your life; be conscious of the lessons and values you are passing on to them

Use your heroes to inspire you to action

Humans have always needed heroes. Heroes inspire us; they help us make sense of the world; they display qualities that we admire and aspire to such as courage, ability to face adversity, to bear sacrifice, to achieve superhuman feats. Our heroes comfort us because they show us that much more can be borne and achieved than we might have imagined possible. We can always be on the lookout for heroes whose stories inspire us on our own journey. We must study their stories and identify the characteristics that helped them succeed. Our heroes should inspire us to action and not mere admiration. We do need, however, to be careful of following a flawed hero; it is devastating to discover our hero has become an anti-hero.

I have always been fascinated by my own heroes. By studying their lives and by analysing the qualities that made them successful, I have learned many important lessons. My heroes—explorers such as Ernest Shackleton, Roald Amundsen, Robert Falcon Scott and Tom Crean—all had a huge passion for what they did, and that passion found expression in a strong self-belief. They were goal-driven, and developed the skills to rise to every challenge and adversity that came their way with courage and humility. I knew that if I emulated my heroes' attributes that I, too, would succeed in achieving my goals.

Shared stories help make sense of who you are and who you can become

If you listen carefully,
at the end you'll be someone else.

Vyasa

Since the beginning of time, human beings have told stories to each other—true stories, imagined stories, even lies. The power of the story or fable is beyond dispute, irrespective of its origins or truthfulness. We never know which story will impact most on us, and how we hear a story depends on how we listen to it. We learn about life from stories that are told orally, that we see on film, that we read in books. They help us make sense of the world and our place in it.

In high-altitude climbing, storytelling is an important and honoured tradition. Each evening climbers gather in a communal camp to listen to and enjoy the stories of people from around the world. Stories are shared and the listeners are entertained and enlightened by what they hear. In this shared storytelling, bonds are formed that cross continents and language barriers.

How we hear depends on how we listen

It was through listening to the stories of other adventurers that I came to know the world. On my first expedition to Mount Everest, in 1993, I was part of an international group of 11 different nationalities whose shared goal was to reach the summit. Each day we would gather for mealtimes in our mess tent. This was when our team shared stories of previous climbs, of their lives, their cultures, their countries and their hopes. This experience gave me the want and the need to explore different countries and to go on the expeditions that I was hearing about.

I hadn't been the most attentive student in geography or history class and didn't even know where some of these places were, but every night at Base Camp I listened, awestruck, and drew up my own bucket list of places I wanted to see. The stories of these explorers inspired my travels which have taken me right around the world to climb the highest points on each of the seven continents and to learn about the traditions and cultures of people wherever I went.

- Share your own stories

- Learn from what you hear

- Be open to stories that challenge your understanding of the world

A hugely successful manifestation of modern-day storytelling is the TED Talks phenomenon whose mission is to spread ideas worth listening to. These talks have become a great learning tool and influencer of people's thoughts and ideas. We all have a story worth hearing but, in the fast-paced world we live in, most of us don't take the time to tell our own or to listen to others' stories. We should, because by listening to stories we learn to push back the boundaries of what we think is possible in life.

 # Who you are today is but one manifestation of who you are capable of being

To be what we are, and to become what we are capable of becoming is the only end in life.

Robert Louis Stevenson

It is usually only when we find ourself in truly testing situations that we find out who we really are and that our authentic self comes to the fore. That being the case, then who are we the rest of the time? We are versions of ourself, wearing a social mask that aids us in our interaction with people and with the world. When we examine how we are with different individuals and different groups, we see that we have a persona which we inhabit and adapt, depending on the situation we are in and the people we are with. In theory, our persona allows us move through our social world more easily and protects our deeper, individual self.

Our flexible persona allows us to express different personality traits at different times. A problem for many of us, though, is that we get too caught up with our persona and begin to think it is who we *really* are. Then our persona becomes rigid and limits our ability to explore who we are capable of becoming. We can find ourself trapped and expected to behave in a certain way, even when we no longer want to do so.

Explore who you can become

Society makes demands as well; if we work in a certain profession, we are expected to dress in a certain way. We accept academics dressing in a way that would be quite unacceptable for a barrister or a doctor. Why is this? Schools have dress codes for their employees—as is the case with innumerable other professions —and teachers are expected not only to abide by the dress code, but also to inhabit the persona those dress codes reflect. Personas make life easier but there is also a danger if we over-identify with them. If we believe that we are the

What is left of you if all you own is taken away?

sum of what we do, earn or own, then we have a hard lesson to learn if these things are taken from us. It is useful to imagine what is left of 'me' if all that I own is taken away.

It is often very hard to break away from the 'person' we have been. People may think we are mad or having some kind of breakdown if we start behaving in a new way, hanging out with a new group, taking up some activity that we previously ignored or disliked. Those who know us may not like these changes. It threatens them and they may be afraid of losing us, or that we are losing 'ourself', but we shouldn't be put off by other people's understanding of who they think we are or should be.

When I first started climbing, I would leave my business in Cork and travel to Kerry wearing a suit, an expensive watch, gold chains and a diamond ring; the hallmarks, as far as I was concerned, of my position in society. My climbing colleagues made fun of these symbols which represented a way of life that they were not part of and didn't value. Initially, this didn't bother me and I continued to display the trappings of my wealth. However, when I first went on expedition to Nepal, I realised that the watch I was wearing could fund the education of 15 children for a year in Kathmandu. I suddenly felt very uncomfortable and this feeling stayed with me on my return home.

Within a short time, I found myself discarding the costly items that had been so important to me but which were now shackling me to a version of myself I no longer wanted to be. My perspective had changed and I was moving away from focusing on material

Express yourself in a new way

acquisition. I had thought that I needed these signifiers of wealth so that people would respect me; I hadn't had the self-confidence to be myself. What climbing and travel taught me was that there was another, more authentic, version of me that I could explore.

Initially, my family found it difficult to understand this change; it was almost as if the man they had known was disappearing in front of their eyes; the man who would only wear suits and stay in plush hotels and who liked to eat out in expensive restaurants was now sleeping in tents and hostels and no longer spending money on stuff to impress others. Whatever money I had, I now used to explore and learn about the world. Gradually, my family came to accept this new expression of myself, but not without a period of adjustment.

Expressing ourself in a new way is something we often do when we move away from our familiar surroundings to somewhere unfamiliar. In a new place, where we know no one and are known by no one, we can experiment with a different version of ourself. It is almost as if we are trying on a new suit of clothes that we haven't worn before. In the journey of life, we should constantly strive to become a better version of ourself so that we are always moving in the direction of becoming the person we are capable of being.

Always remember there is a bigger picture

It is both reassuring and frightening to realise that there is always a bigger picture. It is reassuring in the sense that whatever is consuming us is, in fact, tiny in the grand scheme of things and will lose its significance in the fullness of time. The bigger picture can be frightening when we sense how little control we have over life. Most of us are obsessed with making sense of who we are and what our role in life is. However, if we forget that there is a bigger picture, something much greater than we are, we run the risk of becoming isolated in our understanding of our place in the world.

We may think that everything we do and say is all-important instead of realising that we are passing through this life for a very short period of time. What we do while we are alive is important but it will be absorbed into something vast, way beyond our comprehension. Keeping that reality to the forefront of our mind reminds us to view our position with humility. We are members of communities and it is as members of those communities that we connect with the bigger picture of life. The poet John Donne wrote that, 'No man is an island, entire of itself/

Connect with the bigger picture of life

The world can replenish us in ways we can't even imagine

Every man is a piece of a continent, A part of the main'. We are all part of something bigger, whether we acknowledge it or not, whether we are aware of it or not.

When we acknowledge the bigger picture and actively engage with our participation in it, we connect with the communities we are part of in a more meaningful way. The wider world is full and can replenish us in ways we don't even know when we feel that our world is empty. When we are consumed by a concern, or plan, or emotion, it can take something very small to wake us up and take us beyond that all-consuming state. It helps if we are open to accepting our place in the bigger picture.

When we are drowning in a sea of grief, reconnecting with nature can bring comfort; when we feel that everything is going wrong, we can put our concerns into perspective by thinking of others in far worse situations than ours. By reaching out to others when we are in dire trouble, we can avail of support that we need but don't know exists until we open ourself to accepting that support. By looking at the bigger picture, we come to know that we are not alone; we are part of something much bigger. All that we say and do contributes in some way to shaping the bigger picture. The picture is changing all the time and we are all in it together.

- Remember that there is always a bigger picture

- Take comfort from this fact

- You are important but not all-important

- Everyone else is important too

- Reach out to the wider world to give and offer support

- Be open to the flow of energy that the bigger picture offers

- Become an observer in your own life

I have the power to:

- *Explore and manage my mindset*

- *Explore who I am capable of becoming*

- *Believe in myself*

- *Build strong foundations*

- *Be a great role model*

- *Ask for help*

MINDSET CHALLENGES: HOW TO DEAL WITH THEM

So much of what stops us from achieving what we want in life comes from within ourself and from unhelpful self-talk. We busy ourself creating intricate webs of reasons and excuses for why we can't do this, why we won't do that, and why we shouldn't do something else. We might want something with all our heart but immobilise ourself by procrastinating, or we allow fear to build up to such an extent that we become frozen and unable to act. We allow the prejudice, judgements and criticism of others—and of ourself—to act as obstacles on our route, while shame and stress overpower us so that we want to give up. However, once we decide to deal with these issues and get a proper perspective on them, we can learn how to dismantle and move beyond them.

3

Don't allow procrastination become your default setting

Don't feed unfounded fears

Dismantle prejudice with knowledge

Informed judgements can only be made when you have all the facts

Criticism is always coming your way; find a method of dealing usefully with it

Use shame to motivate you to be your best self

Find a balance between good stress and over-stress

Don't allow procrastination become your default setting

Only put off until tomorrow what you are willing to die having left undone.

Pablo Picasso

When we don't do what we want to do, or what we need to do, or what we intended doing, then we procrastinate. Procrastination has been called the 'thief of time' and that is precisely what it is; we have an objective that we want to reach and yet we stand still—as if suspended in time and space—not moving towards our goal. Everyone experiences procrastination to one degree or another. For some, it's a minor problem that causes inconvenience at times; for others, it's a constant problem that causes much stress and anxiety and prevents us from making a decision or taking action.

Procrastination steals our time

There is any number of reasons why we engage in procrastination, from the glaringly simple to deeply complex psychological ones—everything from laziness to self-doubt and fear can lead us to inaction. The more we procrastinate, the more disillusioned we become, both with the idea and with ourself. The reasons—or excuses—that we give are endless.

- I'm too busy, I'll start tomorrow

- I haven't all the facts

- I can't afford to do it

- I don't have the experience

- I don't know where to start

We like to tell ourself that we are in control and that we can start at any time, ignoring the fact that we are procrastinating. The truth is that we often have negative feelings that we don't want to admit to about what it is we need to do.

- **The project seems too big:** when things are too big, you don't know where to start so you don't start at all. You feel overwhelmed because you believe that the project requires large blocks of time which aren't always available. The truth is that large blocks of time are hardly ever available. If you were asked to eat an elephant you would not be able to eat it in one sitting, but if you eat it one piece at a time, eventually the elephant will be eaten.

- **Fear of failure:** this is the most common reason for procrastination. After all, the safest way not to fail is not to try. Nobody wants to make mistakes so you often feel afraid to start towards your goal for fear of being wrong or failing. Reassure yourself and remember that 'the person who never makes a mistake will never make anything'.

- **Perfectionism:** when you put undue pressures on yourself to be perfect it can make a new task overwhelming. No one expects you to be perfect and neither should you. What's most important is that you make a start. If you wait until everything is perfect, then you will never make the first move or take the first step.

- **Difficult and unpleasant tasks:** when part of achieving your goal is difficult or you don't like the task, you will tend to put off doing it. There is no way around the difficult bits if you want to succeed. Once you get stuck in, the hard task soon becomes a memory on the way to success.

> No one expects you to be perfect; nor should you

What we rob ourself of when we procrastinate is not only time, but our enthusiasm and passion for our goal. We start to doubt ourself and to spend time thinking of reasons why our goal is not achievable. The longer we procrastinate, the more stressed, anxious, disillusioned and helpless we begin to feel. Like all habits, procrastination is one that we can challenge so that we no longer sabotage our desires, wants and goals by putting them off 'because'. It takes honesty, commitment and focus to move from being a serial procrastinator and to become a serial doer.

- **Take action:** all of the great ideas in the world can't beat an average idea that is acted upon. Find a way to do something, anything. Action is essential to overcoming procrastination, even if that action is a small step.

- **Make a plan:** this is often all it takes to move forward when something seems too big, too difficult, or when you're feeling paralysed by perfection. Making a plan gets you going and gives you a direction. Put it down on paper or on a white board, anywhere you can see it right in front of you.

- **Change your motivation:** it's not that you are *not* motivated to do something, it's that you are motivated to do something else. When you view motivation this way, it gives you the choice to make a change. When you find yourself procrastinating, choose to find the motivation to get important tasks done.

- **Enthusiasm:** along with action, enthusiasm is like a secret key to motivate you and abolish procrastination. When you have a hard time feeling enthusiastic, fake enthusiasm until you become fired up again. When you are excited and enthusiastic about something, you are in a position of power and ready to act. Your enthusiasm will fire up those around you. Choose to associate with those who give you constructive feedback in a positive environment.

- **The ten-minute rule:** when you are having difficulty getting started on something, commit to working on it for just ten minutes. Usually this is enough to get going on the project.

- **Why you should start working on your goals today:** good ideas are easy to come by. People often think up the same 'brilliant' idea at the exact same time. The difference between dreamers and people who achieve is that the latter take action. Everyone has the ability, but only a few will actually act.

- **Get an action buddy:** one of the best ways to avoid procrastination and take action on new goals is finding someone to team up with. When you know someone is going to ask you if you did your task, it is more difficult to put off doing it.

- **Find a role model or mentor who has travelled the road before you:** read their books or interviews or, better still, make direct contact with them and ask their advice. Once you share your passion with someone who understands it, it will lessen your self-doubt and fire up your enthusiasm for your goal.

Don't feed unfounded fears

Fear, more than any other emotion, has the capacity to imprison us, restrict our life and stop us from doing what we want to do. Fear is like a mist that infiltrates our mind and stops us from seeing clearly. It is easy to surrender to it and to become immobilised by it. Often, our fear is like a habit, triggered by something or someone. Certain thoughts and behaviours can trigger a fear response even when there is no risk. So fear, while it does serve the vital role of alerting us to danger, also arises in us when there is no danger. Fear is an emotion more often triggered by habitual thinking, memory or imagination than a reaction to a real risk or danger.

Habitual fears include:

- Fear of failure

- Fear of success

- Fear that nothing will ever change

- Fear of change

- Fear of standing out from the crowd

- Fear of being criticised

- Fear of leaving your comfort zone

- Fear of the unknown

- Fear of things that will never happen

When I first decided to climb Mount Everest, I was really scared that I might die. At the time, the statistics showed that one in every ten climbers died on the mountain. Many people advised me against attempting to undertake the climb. They pointed out that I hadn't enough experience and that the challenge was too great. I chose to ignore their advice and decided that instead of focusing on the fact that one in ten climbers on Mount Everest died, I would focus on the statistic that nine out of every ten survived.

I then set about dismantling my fears. I read every account of every ascent of Everest that I could get my hands on. I spoke to every person I could that had already summited the mountain. I learned about the circumstances in which those who hadn't made it back down had died. I found out the exact location of where they had become injured or died, and the reasons why these accidents had happened. With this bank of knowledge, I focused on learning the skills I needed, always keeping to the front of my mind the fact that nine out of every ten climbers returned safely to Base Camp.

My fears diminished and I survived four climbs on Everest because I challenged and dismantled my fears. I adopted the same mindset for all of my other major expeditions, as well as my business and life decisions. Once we have a strategy for dealing with our fears, conquering them gets easier.

Fear, unfortunately, has become a dominant emotion in the world we live in. It is a world where perfection and success

> **Fear stops you from seeing clearly; dismantle your fears**

are narrowly defined and where 'making the grade' is increasingly difficult. Consequently, we fear that we are not good enough. We feel insecure in a society where market forces encourage such feelings and then try and sell us the antidote. In earlier times, our fears were based mainly on physical dangers—humans had to protect themselves against attack and so the 'fight or flight' response developed.

We live in prisons of our own making

Today, most of our fears are in an emotional landscape where we still employ the 'fight or flight' response.

In times of insecurity and doubt, it is easy to allow fear to pervade our thinking and become a habitual response to life and its challenges. When this happens we become incapable of moving, of taking action, of making decisions, and, most vitally, of maintaining hope. When our fears dominate our life, it is as if we are living in a prison of our own making.

The first step in getting out of this prison is to take a breather and give ourself time and freedom to do nothing. The hamster wheel of habitual fear thinking is draining and we need to take time to rest. Then we should look at our fears, one by one, and analyse them in a logical and unemotional way. We can assess how real our fears are and check if they have any foundation in reality. If there is real risk or danger facing us, then we can make practical decisions about what to do.

- Name your fear

- Explore it; ask yourself if it is based in reality; is there, in fact, a serious threat to your safety and security or is the emotion of fear coming from a sense of insecurity and lack of self-belief?

- Be logical in your assessment about why you are feeling fearful

Once we establish the source of our fear and we name it, then we can dismantle it, piece by piece. When fear stops us from living the life that we want to live, we need to be realistic and accept that by letting fear govern our actions—and lack of action—we will live a limited life and never explore the fullness of our potential. On the other hand, when we identify, name and acknowledge that which is feeding our fear, then we can move on from that emotion through logical and rational thinking to re-find our centre of control and courage. If our fears are habitual then we need to start on a journey of positive self-talk where we literally—based on rational thinking—talk ourself out of this emotion.

- Trust yourself

- Ensure you have the skills and knowledge necessary for whatever you are about to undertake

- Gain experience

- Have good people on your team

- Know their level of commitment and loyalty

- Acknowledge your ability and achievements

When we believe in ourself and focus on our goals, fear dissipates and fades away. We move to a place of self-belief and develop the courage to explore our full potential.

Dismantle prejudice with knowledge

In society, we put people into groups in order to make sense of the world around us. This is like a filing system for the brain. It is not based on actual experience or reason, but on some pre-judged idea of what others, who are not part of our group, are like. Prejudicial opinions may be favourable or unfavourable (though usually the latter), although they are not based on actual fact. It is for this reason that we should always be alert for prejudice in ourself and in others. When we experience it towards others, or encounter it towards ourself, we should name it and strive not to get caught up in it.

We can reduce prejudice within ourself or our group by developing empathy and authentic contact with those towards whom we feel prejudice. When we put ourself in the shoes of others, it is easier to see the road they have travelled and where they are coming from. Getting caught up in the prejudices of others distracts us from our focus and wastes energy; we all know the head-banging-off-the-wall

Walk in the shoes of others to understand them

feeling that is part and parcel of arguing against prejudice. We can't always know where people's prejudice is coming from so it's best to keep a cool head and move on.

When I was en route to Everest Base Camp with a group in 1996 we encountered a European trekker who was beating his Sherpa porter with his hand. He maintained that the man was not working hard enough or moving quickly enough. The Sherpa was carrying a heavy pack on his back. The trekker believed that the Sherpa was lazy and some sense of misplaced entitlement allowed him beat the man. I approached the trekker and asked him to stop. He told me that it was none of my business and that the man was 'his' Sherpa. It seemed that, as far as the Sherpa was concerned, the trekker was paying his wages and he had to take what was being meted out to him. One was the perpetrator of prejudice and the other the victim of it.

I have travelled the world on expeditions for almost 30 years and have had the chance to experience life among many different tribes. I have listened to the stories of fellow explorers from countries such as Russia, America, China, Korea, England and Ireland. Although we are each bound by conditioning and tradition, handed down through shared practice and familial connection, I have learned that more unites us than divides us. We are all challenged by success, failure

We are united by much more than that which divides us

and change. We all love, we all get angry, we get hungry, we get tired; we all like to dance and sing. When we move beyond prejudice to see and embrace our common humanity, we find that we are all brothers and sisters in the journey of life.

As individuals, teams, groups, governments and religious leaders, we all have a responsibility to learn how to work together. Creating unity and understanding our differences is key to dismantling prejudice in all areas of life.

Informed judgements can only be made when you have all the facts

Out beyond ideas of wrongdoing and
rightdoing there is a field. I'll meet you there.

Rumi

Judgements are made after all the facts have been presented. The person who has been appointed judge (because they are considered fit for that role due to their training or experience) takes everything into consideration before outlining what they believe to be an impartial, fully informed opinion or judgement. This, in an ideal world, is how the practice of judging should be carried out. The reality is a whole lot different. Most of us have judges in our heads, spouting judgements and handing down virtual sentences on a daily basis. Although we most likely don't have all the facts of the 'case', we go headlong into judgement without a second thought.

Being judgemental and having an opinion are two different things. Judgements are spoken as absolutes that are not open to contradiction. When we express an opinion, we are—implicitly—open to contradiction and to being persuaded that another viewpoint is as valid as—or more valid than—the one we hold. Judging others and the world around us is a habit that is as addictive as smoking is for the committed

A judgemental mindset is like a private prison

smoker, and as harmful to our health. And just as passive smokers can be adversely affected by cigarette smoke, so, too, those subjected to habitual judgements can be trapped by the negative mindset they are exposed to.

The judgemental mindset imprisons both the person who judges and the target of that judgement, trapping everybody in a belief system that is hard to get out of. Giving up the habit of being judgemental is something that we need to work on if we find ourself trapped by our own rigid judging system. We may get a sense of our own moral superiority when we make a judgement, but judging others never makes us truly happy; the opposite, in fact, is true, as we become trapped by our own judgemental mindset. This is a closed mindset, and when we are closed to new learning and experience we cut ourself off from the full experience of what life has to offer.

- Unless you are in possession of all of the facts, realise that your judgements reflect your own limitations, insecurities and fears

- Let go of the habit of seeking perfection

- Accept the brokenness of the world you live in and the people who inhabit it

- Stop trying to change others—it's a waste of your energy (and their patience)

- Start from an attitude of acceptance of people and situations, even if you don't like them and they 'don't come up to your standards'

The key to breaking a judgemental mindset is to open our mind and become interested in the story we are hearing, the context in which it is being told and the person who is telling it. How, we should ask ourself, have they come to this point in their life? When we become open, we become curious. When we explore our curiosity, we learn the full story. And when we know the full story, we are more likely to be less judgemental. We gain a greater understanding of why a situation has arisen and why a person is acting in a specific way.

Judging others is as harmful and addictive as smoking

By respecting the right of others to be different, even if their ways or beliefs aren't ours, we open ourself to change and growth. With greater understanding comes greater empathy. Instead of closing our heart to people, we learn to be open and to connect. This is a much more effective route to changing our world together.

Criticism is always coming your way; find a method of dealing usefully with it

Criticism has earned a bad name over the years; no one wants to be criticised though many of us are ready to be critical of others. If we approach criticism of ourself objectively, if we strive not to take it personally, then we can learn whatever lessons there are to be learned from the critic, especially if the critic is someone we admire. Their concern may be to ensure high standards or good practice. We should view criticism as a free source of feedback while remaining selective about what we decide to take on board.

> **View criticism as free feedback**

There are also those who want to criticise, to find fault and to point out mistakes just for the sake of it; criticising others is like a bloodsport to them. We should look first to the critic and then decide if we want to hear their criticism. If we do, the cardinal rule is to not take it personally. Taking valid criticism on board can help sharpen our focus and make us even more determined to achieve our goal.

- Assess the source of the criticism and decide if it is an informed source whose opinion has merit

- Learn what lessons you can from well-founded criticism

- Don't take it personally

- Don't hold grudges against those who criticise you and don't take on other people's grudges as your own; they are a waste of your time, focus and energy

Use shame to motivate you to be your best self

In the range of human emotions, shame is probably one of the most disliked and least talked about. Nobody wants to feel shame and we don't like witnessing others' shame either. It makes us uncomfortable, probably because when we feel shame it is like a fire burning through us that we can neither extinguish nor hide. Shame makes us feel defenceless and weak so who would want it? Yet, from our earliest years, we are taught about shame. Adults tell children to do this and not to do that in order to avoid doing something shameful. In this way, shame is used as a tool to identify boundaries that adults believe will protect the child.

Shame can be used to identify boundaries

There is a clear distinction between the emotions of guilt and of shame, although the two are related. If we feel guilty about something we have done or said, we know that amends can be made pretty quickly by owning up, apologising and moving on. And that is a key point: there are publicly accepted steps and behaviours for getting rid of our guilt. In fact, the 'guilt' can transfer to the other person if they refuse to accept our apology and they, then, become the 'culprit' and we are seen to be the victim.

Dealing with shame is entirely different, mainly because when we feel shame we identify our entire self with the emotion and the reason for the emotion; it is not that we did something wrong or made a mistake, it is that *we* are wrong. When we feel guilty we can make the decision not to do the same thing again; when we feel shame, we believe that we must change who we are, that we must become a better version of the person we have been.

Shame feels like it could burn us up and destroy us; we want to hide away because, somehow or other, that which we *thought* we were has been violated. We feel shame when we fail, when we believe we haven't

Guilt and shame are different emotions

measured up to what others expect of us and what we expect of ourself, when we are rejected by a person or a group for whatever reason. When we experience shame, we want to disappear or lash out in anger.

I was 29 years of age when, because of feelings of shame, I tried to take my own life. I had been very successful, having left school at 15 and built up a business that I was very proud of. I was a happy-go-lucky, outgoing guy with huge self-belief. I had everything I'd ever wanted—a great family, a big house, nice cars and more money than I required to live very comfortably. Then my bubble burst. I overtraded due to lack of knowledge and was hit, like many other businesspeople, by an economic downturn.

Shame nearly killed me

My wife bankrolled my business with all of her personal savings and agreed that we would mortgage our house to save the business, which I still believed I could salvage.

But I was wrong and lost everything bar the family home. I'd never felt so much shame in my life. I couldn't face family, friends, critics or myself. One night, after another head-wrecking day holed up in my office, I drove my car at speed towards an open wharf. Just before entering the water, my two young sons' faces flashed before me. I jammed on the brakes and, within inches of plummeting into the river, my car came to a halt and I cried uncontrollably.

Shame had nearly killed me. I eventually sought help to deal with my shame and depression through being more open and honest with my family, my employees and the business community. Through my recovery, I discovered that those who loved me had my back and wanted to support me.

Feeling shame is so difficult, inducing shame in others is so despised, and witnessing shame is so uncomfortable that we must ask if there is any value in shame or is it something we should just avoid? Threats of 'You'll shame yourself' if you do such and such or 'You should be ashamed of yourself' if you have done something are used to create boundaries for young people growing up.

Shame can be viewed as an indicator that we want to change

In the same way, shame serves a function in the adult world. As adults, we know what makes us feel ashamed and we try to avoid doing things or acting in a manner that causes us to feel shame and that alienates us from our community or tribe. The threat of shame shows us the boundaries of what is socially acceptable.

While we will never actively seek to shame ourself, we can try and learn something when we do feel it. Studies show that shame can be viewed as an indicator that we want to change. If we can sit with our feeling of shame until the 'burn' of the emotion passes, then we can analyse the distance between who we are and who we want to be. Instead of hiding away or lashing out, we can let the emotion subside before examining where it has come from. Then, with greater understanding, we can work towards lessening that distance between who we want to be and who we have been.

- Avoid toxic shame based on the judgements of others

- Recognise the value of shame as a boundary setter

- Use shame that results from transgressing your own standards as a motivator to become the person you know you can be

Find a balance between good stress and over-stress

Stress occurs when some factor causes us mental, emotional or physical tension and pressure. Sources of stress can be external, coming from the environment or people around us, or internal, arising from illness or disease. When we feel stressed, we react. Reactions include the 'fight or flight' response and range from accelerated heart rate, temperature fluctuation and increased sweating to shaking, loss of muscle control and affected breathing.

Stress encourages us to react

Stress is a word we are all very familiar with but few of us can define easily. It has negative connotations and we spend much of our time trying—and probably failing—to avoid stress. The term, as we understand it, was defined in 1936 by Hans Selye as the 'non-specific response of the body to any demand for change'. The definition has been refined over the following decades and stress is now explained as 'a condition or feeling experienced when a person perceives that demands exceed the personal and social resources the individual is able to mobilise'.

Stress, in the correct proportion, can be a motivating tool to help us achieve goals. Human beings have learned how to adapt to change and threats throughout the ages and it is this highly developed ability that has allowed mankind to survive and thrive when

The things that stress you are different at different times

many other species have disappeared. Stress encourages us to react and adapt; it keeps us on the lookout, so to speak, for our own safety and survival. Finding the right balance, however, between too little, the right amount and too much stress, is not easy. Indeed, we are often over-stressed and suffering the consequences by the time we realise it.

While stressed-out people are everywhere, the things that stress us are different, and what stresses us on one occasion may not stress us at all on another occasion. It is how we approach a situation, our attitude towards it, our preparedness for it and how we are feeling generally, that influences whether or not we find a given situation stressful. The experience of stress is greatly heightened when we feel we are losing control of a situation, irrespective of whether or not this is true. And the opposite is also true; we feel less stressed if we think we are in control, even if, in fact, we are not.

With bad stress, we feel threatened and believe that we cannot control how our day is playing out. Prolonged bad stress can cause depression and suicidal thoughts, and many physical illnesses have been identified as stress related, including heart disease, high blood pressure, asthma, cancer, diabetes and obesity. When we are over-stressed, we tend to engage in bad habits that exacerbate our stress, such as comfort eating, indulging in alcohol and drug use, and turning our back on previously healthy lifestyles. When we react like this, not only do

Take action to challenge over-stress

we fail to reduce the bad stress, we actually exacerbate the situation by becoming the 'threat' in our own life.

We are all susceptible to experiencing over-stress and the fallout from that; it is no respecter of position, age or gender. However, if we have a proactive approach to our physical and mental health, have good nutrition and exercise habits, a solid social network and support group, then we are less likely to experience over-stress. When we are over-stressed, or experiencing bad stress, we need to recognise the symptoms and deal with them as quickly as possible in order to regain balance and avoid more serious consequences. If we take action, we immediately start to challenge the source of the stress and so take back control of the situation.

Exercise helps counter stress

Exercise is recognised as one of the top ways to counter stress. Because stress induces immediate physical responses in the human body, we can counter those responses by physically moving our bodies to regain our chemical balance. Learning how to switch off and relax effectively and healthily is also vital. I have learned the benefits of walking away from stressful situations and totally immersing myself in a completely different, unrelated environment.

During one of the worst periods of my life, a friend asked me to go hillwalking. I thought he was mad. I told him I was a workaholic and not a walkaholic and that I needed to stay focused on solving my business problems. His persistence, however, wore me down and I agreed. I reluctantly joined a group of seasoned hillwalkers to climb a 2,400ft mountain in County Kerry. The physical effort demanded that I concentrate on putting one foot in front of the other. That, and the focus of a new goal—the summit—forced me to think about what I needed to do to get to the top of that mountain. For the first time in months I wasn't thinking about the financial mess I was in. When

Learn not to feed your stress

I returned to work, I found my mind was clearer and I was able to focus better.

The following week, I climbed Carrauntuohil, Ireland's highest mountain at 3,414 feet, and enthusiastically declared that I was going to climb Mount Everest. That turning point not alone helped me deal with my stress and develop the skills I needed to rebuild my business, it also set me on a life-changing adventure that has taken me all around the world.

Taking part in sports, meditation, travel or just taking time out helps to relieve negative stress. We all need to get away from the hustle and bustle of day-to-day living and allow our brain time out. When we are stressed we often feed our stress instead of starving it; we sit with it instead of moving away from it to focus on other things that bring positivity into our life.

When you are over-stressed:

- Move physically away from the source of stress, even for short periods of time

- Take time out for a break and to get a proper perspective

- Find a good support group

- Exercise—walk, run, climb, practise yoga

- Immerse yourself in something else

- Do something that you normally enjoy even if it is the last thing you feel like doing

- Take a few days off

Generally we should try and order our life so that excessive stress is minimised. A strong foundation is immensely helpful in dealing with the stresses that will inevitably come our way.

To balance stress in life build and maintain:

- A good social network

- A good working routine

- A regular, positive social life

- A determination to work smart and not long

- Daily exercise

- Good nutrition

- Sufficient sleep on a regular basis

Stressful events will always happen; we can't stop them but what we can do is ensure that we are as prepared as possible to deal with stress and that we use good stress to motivate us to learn how to deal with challenges.

I have the power to:

- *Decide what I truly want*
- *Tackle my fears*
- *Accept people for who they are*
- *Not take criticism personally*
- *Be comfortable with myself*
- *Adapt to change*

EXPLORE YOUR WANTS: BELIEVE IN YOURSELF

Before we start on any journey, we need to tap into our authentic wants, the ones that really mean something to us as opposed to the ones imposed on us by others. Once we have identified them, we should explore our wants and let them find shape in our dreams, visualising what they will be like in reality. Our passion fuels our dreams, while our ambition and motivation, allied with a healthy self-belief, become the vehicle by which our wants find expression in the full realisation of our dreams.

4

Know what you want

Dream and dream big

Visualise your best life

Passion fuels your want

Ambition helps you keep your focus on what you want

Check in regularly on your motivation level

Practise self-belief

Know what you want

Want is the most important ingredient in helping us identify and pursue our goals. Without want, it is impossible to move forward. Our goals come into clear view when we act on our wants. We shouldn't feel guilty about what we want. We must be fearless about it; we must give ourself permission to feel it, to express it and pursue it. Want experienced in a physical way is like a hunger and when we experience this hunger we need to ask ourself what exactly it is we are willing to do to feed it.

To know what we want we have to get in touch with who we really are, and who we are is made up of many parts—some inherited, some adopted and some learned during our life. When we are born, our parents bestow their wants and dreams for us on our very young shoulders. They want us to have a good life, to be happy, to achieve. Part of our inheritance from them is their dreams for us.

One of the strongest forces shaping our wants is the market. Sophisticated and smart advertising creates worlds and sells us better versions of ourself inhabiting these worlds. We live in a market-driven society that is constantly trying to sell us stuff. The best way to sell something is to convince people that they want it and a good salesperson knows all the tricks of the trade to achieve this. We buy what they are selling because we are told this is what we want, this is what we should be wearing, this is the car we should be driving to match the job we should have and the lifestyle we should aspire to.

None of this—neither what we inherit from our parents, nor what society tells us we should want, nor what the market is trying to sell us—is necessarily what we *truly* want, although, in many cases, we embrace our inherited wants and happily make them our own. Our parents,

> To know what we want we have know who we are

our communities, society and the market have their own agenda, but if we don't ever investigate what it is we really want ourself, then we will never be able to truly engage with our own unique abilities.

Sometimes, the wants and dreams that others have for us may feel like burdens that we feel obliged to carry. It is hard to throw other people's dreams aside, especially when we love them and they love us and only want the best for us. In fact, we may be quite happy to live out the dreams we inherit, and add to them as we go along. We must, however, recognise that each one of us has the right to choose our own path in life and we need to give ourself permission to do just that.

Once we have given ourself permission to tap into our want, we need to experience it even if that experience causes us pain and heartache. Without feeling the true depth of our want, of our hunger for a better life for ourself, we won't take the steps necessary to meet that want.

You have the right to choose your own path

Sometimes we turn away from feeling the true nature of what we want because we are frightened by what it will take to feed it. We find it easier to let our desire for something go unexplored, to let it simmer away over the years rather than let it boil over into something passionate and huge that could have life-changing consequences.

We may also feel that we will be overwhelmed by the strength of our want if we allow ourself to fully experience it. This fear shouldn't be a barrier preventing us from experiencing the full force of our want. We should check how badly we want something and what we are willing to do to get it. Then, if we truly believe it is in our best interest, we should go after it with passion, tenacity and self-belief.

- Want has to have an objective

- Want has to be followed by action if your goal is to be reached

- Be clear about how much you are willing to feed your want with passion, action and commitment to see it realised as a goal

One of the most frequent questions I am asked is how I and the teams I lead and work with have been so successful in achieving our major goals in business and adventure over the last 30 years. It all comes down to knowing what we want and taking action to fulfil that want. My mother, Bina, who is another great mentor of mine, gave me a verse about the attributes required to succeed in making what you want reality. I keep it with me at all times and when I doubt myself or my commitment to achieve I read it.

If you want a thing bad enough to go out and fight for it,
You must give up your time, your peace and sleep for it,
If your life seems so lonely and useless without it
And all that you dream and plan is about it,
If gladly you fret for it, then sweat for it
Then you must go for it,
But go for it with all of your capacity, strength and tenacity.
If you simply go after the things in life you really want
Though tired, gaunt and lonely and if,
Day after day, you besiege and beset it
You will get it.

These lines have been a rallying call and a source of inspiration to me for many years. By following its directive—to pursue what we want with all of our capacity, strength and tenacity—we can stay focused and achieve much.

What do you want?

- To be a better parent, daughter, son, sister, friend, partner, colleague?

- To be someone who can take life in their stride?

- To live a life of adventure?

- To be open to change?

- To make money?

- To leave a legacy that you can be proud of?

- To become more open to learning new skills?

- To make new friends?

- To travel?

- To become more compassionate?

- To create employment?

- To give back to your community?

- To buy a new car?

- To have better health?

- To find a partner?

Make your list once you have identified what it is that *you* want. Then be hopeful. The poet Seamus Heaney wrote: 'Even if the hopes you started out with are dashed, hope has to be maintained.' Hope can be described as want allied with the expectation that what we want will come true. Hope cherishes your want and is essential for the human spirit to survive.

- Examine your inherited wants

- Identify your own wants

- Give yourself permission to truly feel them

- Give yourself permission to express them

- Allow your wants to become your passions

- Be fearless in exploring and owning your wants

Dream and dream big

Once we have allowed our want to grow within us, what next? What do we do with this passion that has been unleashed within? We let it flow into our dreams and see where it takes them and us. We give ourself permission to dream about what we want to do, where we want to go, the things we want to achieve, the person we want to become. We shouldn't be ashamed or embarrassed by our dreams—they are the expression of our wants. We need to have the courage to tell people what we want and what our dreams are; we should stick with what we know is our heart's desire, no matter what the reaction of others is.

- Observe the *you* in your dreams: how does this version of you feel and act in your dream life?

- Do you *want* to give expression to this version of yourself?

- If your dreams are different from the dreams others have for you, or if they are new dreams for a new life, let the dream take hold in your imagination and grow

I left school at 15 years of age to become a millionaire. I had a hunger to be successful and a want for the trappings that I believed would bring happiness to me and my family. Even though I was a bricklayer from a working-class background, I dreamed about owning a big house and expensive car, and having the money to travel and fund a comfortable lifestyle. When I told people about my dream, they laughed; they ridiculed me and tried to put me down but I persisted in my conviction that my dream would come true. I ignored

Allow yourself to dream

their taunts and succeeded in achieving my goal by the time I was 23.

Whenever I tap into an authentic want, I allow it into my subconscious so that it shapes my waking dreams and, in a short time, there are clear pictures in my mind of what I want; the 'want' starts taking shape in the freedom of the dream landscape.

Following a big dream allows us see that there are many versions of ourself that we can be. We can evolve into these new versions once we give permission to our wants and dreams to find full expression in our mind. 'Dreaming big' allows us to have bigger expectations of what we can achieve. Whatever the limit of our expectations, what we achieve will reflect this. Many of us only dream within our comfort zone, never pushing ourself to our full potential. So we should dream and dream big but, most importantly, we shouldn't leave our dreams in the recesses of our mind. They need to be brought into our daytime dreaming and given life.

I will never forget how disappointed I was when I reached the age of 18 and was still far from achieving my dream of becoming a millionaire. I was going through a period of doubt and started questioning my ability, commitment and desire to achieve my objective. Simply put, I started listening to my negative self-talk and became frustrated. I needed reaffirmation and encouragement to stay focused so I went for advice to my father, who is my hero and mentor, and asked if I should give up on my dream. His response amazed me. 'Son, you are a dreamer,' he said, 'so dream and dream big, but remember, it's in the following of the dream that the success lies. Let achieving it be a bonus.' I have used his wise counsel throughout my life and have enjoyed both the efforts and rewards involved in pursuing my dreams.

A big dream allows us to go on a journey of exploration, adventure, failure and success. We are all ordinary people capable of achieving extraordinary things and the first place we achieve the extraordinary is in our dreams.

- Have extraordinary dreams

- Feed your dreams with your wants

- Allow your dreams have full expression in your mind

- Don't be embarrassed by your dreams

- Don't let other people's reactions to your dreams put you off; they don't yet see the picture that you see in your mind

Visualise your best life

It takes many words to describe what a single image can present. Images are powerful; they transport us immediately to another place and allow us the freedom and space to explore our response. An integral part of planning and goal-setting is visualisation or imagining what we want looks like. With powerful, free-flowing visualisation we also experience what we want feels like. In fact, we can almost taste it.

Once we identify what we want, it is an automatic reflex to create an image of it in our mind. If, for example, we want to build an extension to our house, the first thing we do is look at images of extensions and then our brain gets to work, modifying and personalising these images until we see, perfectly formed, the extension that we want. If we are invited to a formal event we picture what we will wear and how we will look well in advance of the event and do whatever we need to do to achieve that 'look'.

Visualisation is an integral part of goal-setting

Every time I set myself a big goal, I get a picture of what I want to achieve, frame it and put it in my hallway or bedroom so that every day I see it. It's in my face and it keeps me focused. When I was 16, I saw a photograph of a beautiful house. I decided this was the kind of house I wanted for my family and, by the time I was 23, I was living in a replica of the house I'd seen at 16.

Once I set the goal of climbing Mount Everest—after only my second ever mountain climb—I hung a picture of the world's highest mountain in my hallway and looked at it several times a day. Seven years later I was standing on its summit. Visualisation has been an integral part of achieving every one of my goals. It is one of the greatest tools we can use to develop a closer relationship with our goals to allow them to inhabit our mind and memory thereby driving us on to success.

Clearly picture what you want

We visualise every day. When we feel hungry, we visualise what we would like to eat. When we feel cold, we fantasise about warm clothes and heat. When we want something significant, we really need to visualise what it looks and feels like. It's easy to do this for our smaller, daily wants—such as how relieved we'll feel when we get out of the traffic jam and home to a nice meal—but it takes more effort and focus to visualise a big, life-changing goal, something that we want viscerally and need to make sense of.

Feel what your new life will be like

This is when we need to take the time to imagine our want in its realised form—what it looks like, what it feels like, how we feel about it, how we are in this version of our life. If, for example, we want to own a new car because we are fed up with always having a second-hand car, before we ever think about how we are going to afford a replacement, we need to visualise the new one.

- What does it look like?

- What colour is it?

- What make is it?

- What does it feel like to drive?

- How do I feel when I am driving it?

- What am I wearing when I am driving it?

Soon the picture is complete. This process should be applied to everything we want and dream about. Once we visualise our goal, we must keep that image in our head and look at it regularly so that we don't forget what it looks like. The more familiar we become with the image, the more integrated its presence becomes in our life and the closer its realisation becomes. When we have a full visualisation of what our want looks like in its final form, this image helps us as we journey towards achieving our goal. When the going gets tough and we become unfocused or despondent, the image of our goal helps us refocus.

A clear picture of what you want helps keep you focused

- When you want something, visualise it; fill in the picture until it is complete

- See what you look like in this visualisation

- Note how you feel

- Look at the picture often

- When your plan is not going well, visualise your goal to help you refocus

Passion fuels your want

We say that we are passionate about something when we bring a strong emotional energy to the activity or process. There are many things we do in life that we are not passionate about but that we must do for one reason or another. When, however, we do something that we are passionate about, it's an entirely different ball game; the world is a different colour when we are ignited by our passion.

Work seems easier because our enthusiasm helps us through the difficult parts; we don't resent the time spent on activities that we love whereas we might resent every single minute spent doing something we don't like. This is why we are always encouraged to work at something that we love—our passion makes things easier to do. We learn more easily if we are passionate about the subject because our focus is on where our passion is taking us and challenges seem less daunting.

> **Passion colours our world with energy**

I have met many passionate people in my life but one that stands out is Ger McDonnell, a climber from County Limerick. In January 2002, when I first met Ger, I was blown away by his passion and enthusiasm. At the time, I was planning to return to Mount Everest to attempt its summit from the south side in Nepal. An employee asked if I would meet with Ger, a friend of hers. He was on a visit home from Alaska, where he lived and worked, and he wanted to meet me to talk about climbing Mount Everest.

I had already picked my team but agreed to meet him. When he arrived at the expedition office, his passion for climbing was palpable. In addition, Ger had one of the most infectious smiles I had ever seen.

> ## It is hard to resist the passion of others

From the moment we shook hands, I felt a bond between us. His opening remarks were: 'Hi, I'm Ger, I love climbing, I'm self-sufficient and I have been training for the last few years on big mountains in Alaska. I believe I would be a great addition to your Everest team. I know you won't be disappointed and I'll make you proud.'

I was blown away by his passion, his sincerity and his self-belief, which made me really want to connect with him. The following morning, I rang Ger to say I would love for him to join my team. He reached the summit of Mount Everest on our expedition in 2003. Sadly, he died in 2008 while climbing K2, the second highest mountain in the world.

The energy of someone who is ignited by passion is hard to resist. When we find people who are passionate about the same things as us, it is a joy to share that passion. Passionate people attract other

> ## See your passion as fuel for your goal

passionate people who are willing to help them achieve their goals. Mentors, role models and heroes will rally to help us achieve our dreams if we have passion.

When our passion for something is ignited we must match it with the necessary skills and rational understanding to reach our goal. Allowing ourself to be overwhelmed by an undisciplined passion can be destructive. We should think of our passion as fuel for our dreams and goals that keeps our skills, training and discipline going, especially when we feel we want to stop.

- Ignite your passion for something

- Share that passion with like-minded people

- Balance your passion with skills, training and discipline

- Use your passion as a fuel

Ambition helps you keep your focus on what you want

Ambition is our desire to accomplish and achieve in our life. It sometimes gets a bad name; people who are ambitious are often considered ruthless and selfish, but we need ambition to help us focus our wants and dreams into something concrete. Ambition is like an accelerator and, the stronger it is, the faster we travel. There are, of course, dangers in travelling too fast so we need to use our ambition carefully if we want to avoid getting into a situation where things get out of control.

The first thing we need to do is identify our ambition, take ownership of it and not allow it be curtailed by others. Ambition, allied with self-belief, the correct skills for the task

> Ambition is our desire to accomplish and achieve

at hand and proper focus will keep us achieving throughout our life. Ambition that is not balanced by those elements can be dangerous; without the proper checks, our ambition can accelerate and we can find ourself blinded by it and entering the danger zone where we can no longer calculate risk and where the stakes are too high.

- Have ambition

- Don't let your ambition run away with you

- Balance your ambition with self-belief, skills and focus

Check in regularly on your motivation level

Motivation is our desire or willingness to do something. Our level of motivation determines how we will act; basically, if we want something

Monitor your motivation level and work to keep it high

badly enough we will do what we can to get it. If our desire isn't that great, we might make some attempt but won't be too fussed about the end result. If we were highly motivated all the time for all our undertakings, we could end up burning ourself out. On the other hand, if we don't tap into our motivation then we miss

out on many things that will enhance our life.

Our motivation level may go up and down at different times and external factors can strongly influence our general level of motivation. Therefore, it is important that we check that level, especially if we are undertaking something important. It is so much harder to achieve something—or even take part in something—if we are not sufficiently motivated. But when we are motivated we are goal-focused and it is this focus that helps keep our motivation level high. When it is high, the journey is more enjoyable and the challenges along the way more manageable.

When we are highly motivated to achieve or complete something, we are energised and focused in our behaviour. We are organised and efficient with our time. For example, when we are going on holiday and have a lot of tasks to complete before we head off, we are usually

Self-motivators can achieve more in day-to-day life

very motivated to get that work done before the deadline. Without the holiday to focus us, the same work could take a lot longer to do.

As self-motivators, we can achieve a lot more in our day-to-day life. To do this, we need to be realistic, have an identifiable goal and reward ourself when we reach it. If we do

this, we learn how to activate and maintain our personal motivation level. Whether we are doing something because we want to, or because we have to, our motivation level is often what will see us over the line.

To activate and maintain your motivation level:

- Set yourself a goal or challenge

- Create a time-frame

- Be realistic about what needs to be done to achieve the goal

- Mark milestones along the way; this can be as simple as a tea break when you reach a certain point in the process

- Celebrate when you reach the end point

Highly motivated people are comfortable in their ability to see something through, no matter what. When we are motivated, we are willing to face challenges head-on because we have self-belief, energy and focus. Our level of motivation plays a crucial role in determining our chances of succeeding so we should look after it and ensure it's where it needs to be for whatever we need to do.

Practise self-belief

Man often becomes what he believes himself to be. If I keep on saying to myself that I cannot do a certain thing, it is possible that I may end by really becoming incapable of doing it. On the contrary, if I have the belief that I can do it, I shall surely acquire the capacity to do it even if I may not have it at the beginning.

Mahatma Gandhi

We are capable of doing what we believe we are capable of doing. The opposite is also true: we are not capable of doing that which we don't believe ourself capable of doing. We may *actually* be capable of doing it, but consistent lack of belief in our ability to do it undermines that very

Be the last to give up on yourself

ability to the point where it is lost or lessened.

The American industrialist Henry Ford once said, 'Whether you think you can or think you can't, you're right'. It is the same mantra that my grandmother repeated to me when she was teaching me how to work a business at the young age of six. So the issue is not really about capability (because we can learn most things) but self-belief.

We need to believe in ourself; if we don't, then we are really stacking up the odds that we won't achieve our goals even if we are capable of doing so. Without belief that we can do something, doing it becomes very difficult indeed. It is an advantage if we are lucky enough to meet someone who believes in us and our dreams, but we must be the first to believe and the last to give up on ourself. Self-belief, like positivity, is something that we need to practise regularly.

When we have self-belief and confidence to achieve what we set out to do, we also need to beware of becoming overly confident in our own ability. We don't want to lose sight of the fact that we always need to expect the unexpected and to remember that things are ever-changing.

- Practise positive self-talk

- Find a mantra that becomes your personal prayer and say it as often as you need to, especially if doubt begins to take hold

- Get the necessary skills and training to give yourself every opportunity to succeed

- Find good mentors

- Tap into your wants

- Get rid of bad habits that undermine your ability to fulfil your capabilities

In May 2004, dawn was breaking in the Himalaya as my climbing partner Clare O'Leary and I approached the final push towards the summit of Mount Everest. As darkness turned to light, we came across a body in the ice. We presumed it was Scott Fischer, the American climber and guide who had died in 1996. His remains were a reminder of the dangers of the area we were in. We were travelling in the Death Zone, the point on the mountain above 8,000m where the amount of oxygen is insufficient to sustain human life. It was -35 degrees Celsius and we were exhausted. The sight of the dead body gnawed at our belief that we could get to the summit and safely back down again.

This was a crux moment and we had a decision to make: to continue or to retreat. We stopped and looked at each other as we mentally assessed our situation. We had

Self-doubt can afflict even the most confident of us

done the preparation, the training and the research. We knew we could do it. Thumbs went up and we continued, believing not only that we had the ability to make it to the summit, but also to get back without paying the ultimate cost. This type of self-belief is required when we are pursuing our dreams. Clare went on to become the first Irish woman to climb Mount Everest and to climb each of the Seven Summits with me, a feat we completed in 2005.

If we don't nurture self-belief, we expose ourself to the danger of falling into self-doubt, low self-esteem and procrastination. In fact, self-doubt can afflict even the most confident of us at certain times in our life. It could be that we are at a low energy ebb, or our emotions are raw and we feel vulnerable. We need to see it as something to be managed. What is vital is that we do not fuel self-doubt with negative self-talk that can eat into our self-confidence and deflect us from our goals.

Have faith; focus on your goal

At these times, we must try and become an observer of ourself. We should ask if there is any real reason why we shouldn't go ahead with our next action. If there is a real reason not to proceed, then we need to deal with that. But if we remain in a place of doubt, we will never progress. We have to have faith and focus on the goal; we must remember all the preparation and training already done, and the milestones already achieved along the way. We must stand back, observe our emotions and apply logic to the situation.

When we suffer a crisis of self-confidence in ourself, starting to achieve, even if the achievement is tiny, will help rebuild our self-belief. Success in anything automatically builds self-belief and helps us refocus.

- You might have all the skills and ability in the world but if you don't have self-belief you will not succeed

- Succeed where you can so that your self-belief is growing all the time

- Match your self-belief with thorough training and hard work

- Be the last person to give up on yourself

I have the power to:

- *Dream big*

- *Be extraordinary*

- *Visualise what I want*

- *Set myself achievable goals*

- *Ignite my passion*

- *Achieve my ambitions*

TAKE ACTION, SET YOUR GOAL, MAKE A PLAN

When we want to achieve something, to change something or to create something new, we must make a decision and take action. No matter what the first step is, no matter how big or how small, the important thing is that we take action. This helps us to see our goal more clearly and, once we have that clarity, we absolutely have to make a plan that has a beginning, middle and end as well as a realistic time-frame. Choice and opportunity are around us all the time; they may not be perfect but they are what we need to grab right now to help us take those first vital steps in becoming active agents in making our dreams reality.

5

Make a decision and act

Identify your goals clearly

Make a plan

Examine your options and choose the best from what is available

Opportunity is everywhere: learn how to identify it

Time is not endless; plan yours and use it wisely

Make a decision and act

In any moment of decision, the best thing you can do is the right thing, the next best thing is the wrong thing, and the worst thing you can do is nothing.

Theodore Roosevelt

No matter what our options are in any given situation, we should always decide to do something. We should never decide to do nothing. When we decide to act, we focus on what is possible at that given moment; the choices might not be great, in fact, they might be the opposite. Nonetheless, we should make a decision and act. If we don't, we abdicate from being an active agent in our own life and find ourself in a position where we lose all sense of control. There are, of course, times in our life when we have no control over what is happening but it is seldom that we can't take action and make an active contribution.

We should never decide to do nothing

We make many decisions on a daily basis; we decide what to wear, what to eat, how to spend our time, who to hang out with. When it comes to the bigger things in life, however, we often find it hard to decide what to do. There might be a lot at stake—making the wrong decision might carry a high risk; it might even be dangerous. But if we decide to do nothing and wait to see what happens, it is then that we can find ourself in the worst possible situation.

I found myself imprisoned by inaction when I was 29 and my property business collapsed. I was totally shocked by the situation I found myself in: I was going broke due to a mixture of overtrading, inexperience and a general financial crisis in the country. I had massive borrowings and the bank was demanding the sale of our family home. My self-esteem was at an all-time low. I lost all confidence and belief in myself. I was embarrassed that I could not pay the creditors who had been so loyal to me over the years. I was devastated and traumatised. I felt I couldn't make proper decisions and, therefore, I didn't do anything about my problems. I ran away from my responsibilities by going into denial about the fact that I was broke.

Worse still, I blamed everyone else for my mistakes. Not knowing what to do, and afraid to take any action, I put my head in the sand like an ostrich. I went to work every day for more than a year in fear of what was going to go wrong next, and things continued to go wrong. Following a suicide attempt, I realised that inactivity and feeling sorry for myself was not the way to go. With help from family and colleagues, I changed my attitude and took action. I went to the bank and re-negotiated a plan to help me trade out of my difficulties.

Without focus, we feel we have no influence over our future

I explained my position to my creditors and they rallied behind me. Not one of them took advantage of my downturn or bid when my properties went up for sale. They felt that they, too, could have ended up in the same position. I had actively asked for help and received it. Everyone co-operated and helped me to rebuild my business because I had taken action and was honest about my situation. Three years later, all my debts were paid off because I had—eventually—chosen action over inaction.

Waiting without focus or engagement eats away at our confidence and allows fear to take hold. When we are without focus, we feel we have no influence over our future. If, on the other hand, we make a decision, we stay actively involved and we make things happen. What happens may not be what we ideally want, but, by engaging in the decision-making process, we move away from inactivity, stasis and procrastination.

Action signifies a statement of intent to ourselves and the world

If we have a very big goal or dream that we want to achieve, we can start moving towards that goal by deciding to take even a small action. This action signifies a statement of intent to ourself—and to others—that we have made a decision and we are acting. It may take a while to achieve what it is we want but, by making a decision to do something, we are taking a step in the direction of that goal, and each step we take brings us closer to it.

Identify your goals clearly

It must be borne in mind that the tragedy of life doesn't lie in not reaching your goal. The tragedy lies in having no goals to reach.

Benjamin Mays

To start any journey, we need a destination—the place to which we are travelling. When we understand and embrace our life as a journey of adventure, our 'destination' becomes the goals we set for ourself. No matter how many goals we have, or what size they are, the goal is always the destination. Without a destination, there is no point in starting the journey; without a destination we don't know where we are going or why we are moving in the direction in which we are heading.

> To start any journey, we need a destination

I have a system for all my own major goals. Whenever I set myself a challenge, I write it down. I commit it to paper and, in this way, I make a commitment to myself to make it happen. The goal is summarised clearly in one sentence. I have used this simple formula for goals in my personal, business and family life. As soon as I know that I'm close to completing one goal, I set myself the next one. I am constantly rejuvenated, energised and excited by having rolling goals as I move from one challenge to the next.

Identifying and setting goals is vital if we want to fully engage in exploring our potential. Each day we should engage with the process of taking an action to move in the direction of achieving something small while remaining focused on our major goal. If we don't stay engaged, we can drift off course and lose our direction and focus. Our level of achievement is much higher when we have clear and identifiable goals. If we imagine what reaching our goals

> Start to explore your potential

will feel like, how we will react and the emotions we will experience when we get to our 'destination', it makes the goal more achievable and more tangible.

We can have multiple goals at any one time but it is better not to have too many as it becomes difficult to maintain the focus and energy needed to complete them. It is better to have a small number of big goals and to view our journey as a road of milestones to be reached as we make our way to the big goal.

Our goals should be ambitious. Those that are within easy reach don't challenge our imagination or our ability. We need to step outside our comfort zone and seek to reach our full potential with ambitious goals. We can break these down into measurable and realistic milestones which become our short-term goals. With meaningful long, medium and short-term goals, we apply and test our potential. Another advantage of having bigger goals is that it usually takes a longer time to reach them; this time allows us the opportunity to learn new skills and have new experiences along the way.

We need to step outside our comfort zone

The process of climbing high-altitude mountains always has to be broken down into a series of milestones. Otherwise, the sheer vastness of the undertaking would overwhelm the climber. Once the mountain is broken down into smaller 'mountains', it becomes manageable and more achievable. We mark milestones along the way and, as we reach each one, we make a point of acknowledging how far along the road we have travelled and assess what we have achieved to that point. Each milestone reached is a goal in and of itself and a component of the bigger goal.

Having climbed Mount Everest four times and reached the summit twice, I have learned well the lesson of breaking down a big goal into smaller goals. On Everest, these were the years of training before departure, the journey to Base Camp, and getting to Camps One, Two, Three and Four. Each milestone brought me closer and closer to achieving the ultimate goal of reaching the summit of Everest and surviving.

There will always be obstacles

There will always be challenges and obstacles on the journey towards our goals; this is the experience of everyone who has ever set a worthwhile goal. What matters is that we don't give up or change the goal when the going gets tough. If necessary, we change the route but we must always move in the direction of our goal. If we find that we are in a rut that holds us back, we need to keep our focus firmly on the goal; we need to keep seeing it and feeling what it will be like to achieve it and, eventually, we will get back on track.

The goal itself has to remain all-important and we can't allow obstacles, criticism or setbacks to deflect us from it. If we do, then we will never fulfil our potential. To help us remain focused it helps to 'travel light'; in mountain climbing this means not carrying extra equipment that will weigh us down or hold us back. In daily life, it means we need to ensure that we don't carry mental 'weight' in the form of negative thinking, excessive

> By travelling light, we keep focus on our goals and what is truly important

and unnecessary decision making, or the taking on board of unhelpful criticism. We avoid carrying 'weight' by not having too many goals or distractions that weigh us down and take us from our main focus.

Paring back and de-cluttering allows us create space for what is truly important. It also allows us to see more clearly the route we need to take. When we get rid of anything we don't need or use—be it physical stuff or bad habits—we have fewer decisions to make and, consequently, can focus more on what we want to do and where we want to go. Our body and mind function better when we travel light and only carry what we need for our journey. We have more energy and fewer responsibilities which helps us to be more efficient.

Sometimes, our goals are shared objectives, with maybe a small number of people working on a project or with a larger group, such as a sports team. In this situation, each of us must recognise the intrinsic importance of the role played by each and every person. Everybody on a team plays a role and without the contribution that each makes—no matter what it is—reaching the goal will be much harder.

> Everybody on the team plays a role

When we are part of a group with a shared goal, we all need to be aware of the collective vision of how we will reach our goal. In other words, we must all work in unison towards a recognisable and shared objective. All the team members must know and abide by the ethos of the team, and personal issues should be kept in the background. When the stakes are high, the team members must recognise this and bow to the common cause which is the shared goal.

When we reach our goal, it is important to ensure we have another in the pipeline. Why? Because the exploration of our potential is a lifelong journey and while we must take time to celebrate goals achieved, we must always ask ourself, 'What's next?'.

Make a plan

Our goals can only be reached through a vehicle of a plan, in which we must fervently believe, and upon which we must vigorously act. There is no other route to success.

Pablo Picasso

Once we identify and set our goals, the next step is to make a plan. Goals remain as ideas and dreams until we tie them down into concrete, realistic plans that have a beginning, middle and end. So, once we know what our goals are, we need to sit down and draw up a plan, literally going through all the details and specifics of what needs to be done to achieve our goal.

Planning is crucial to success and if we don't plan properly, we run the risk of almost certain failure. All successful individuals, teams and companies that have ambitious goals and targets have a plan of action on how to achieve them. They set their goals, form a strategy and then they develop a plan. If the team is not informed of the plan, individuals will go in different directions and, at best, create chaos and inefficiency and, at worst, ensure the failure of the project. Having a plan is crucial to having a controlled and efficient way of succeeding in achieving our goals.

Set goals, form a strategy, develop a plan

Good planning helps keep us focused. The act of creating a plan helps us mentally and physically because it anchors us and demands that we start engaging with the process. A plan is like the itinerary for a journey. When we set out on a big adventure we always ensure that we plan and know our itinerary, that we have a good map, the clothes we need and enough money to cover our costs. We read up on any potential dangers, we get travel and health insurance. Basically, we do everything to ensure we have the best possible chance of having a successful journey where dangers are minimised and enjoyment is maximised.

We need to be equally rigorous when it comes to planning our goals. We should know where we are going and how we are going to get there; we need to know how long it will take and how much it will cost. The more prepared we are, the more enjoyable the journey, even when it is difficult and challenges present themselves.

We need to know the nature of what is ahead and be honest in our appraisal of how ready we are to set out on this journey. If we are not ready yet, then we can take the necessary steps to get to the required state of readiness. This might mean training,

> **Do everything to give yourself the best chance of succeeding**

getting fit, upskilling, learning a new language, creating a network, or working more on our mindset. Whatever it is, preparing ourself adequately is an integral part of the planning process.

Another important component at the start of the planning process is acceptance of what our starting point is. We need to be strict with ourself and honestly assess our ability, skills, commitment, discipline and financial situation. Once we assess and accept where we are right now, then we know our starting point. Whatever that point is, it is vital to remember it is *our* starting point. It doesn't matter what anyone else's is; we don't start our holidays from anyone else's house nor do we start planning our goals from anyone else's starting point.

We need to check in on our progress on a regular basis so that we can adjust anything that needs adjusting as external or internal conditions change. We can always tweak our plan while maintaining focus on our goal. We do, however, run a risk if we deviate from our plan and go off on an unknown route—we might be lucky and still arrive at our destination, but the risk of not getting there is certainly higher if we travel an unplanned route.

Regular assessment also allows us the opportunity to check in on our personal habitual derailers—those actions that keep pulling us back into a rut and

> **Habitual derailers keep us in a rut and impede progress**

impeding our progress. For example, not starting our day at the time we have decided can throw our entire plan off course if we allow it. We might think 'I've lost that half hour, what's the point in trying to do all that I had planned for today?'. But there will always be days where we don't start at the wished-for time, and a day rarely goes by without some unexpected interruption. We need to observe our reaction to these derailers and learn to deal with them in a constructive way.

If we are rigid in our planning, then our plan can be broken whereas if we are fluid (and this does not mean lax and lazy) then we can incorporate the inevitable unplanned-for events that are, in fact, an integral part of life. Once our commitment to our goal and our focus remains strong, then our habitual derailers will eventually lose their power and disappear as we become energised by our progress. Our goals are like seeds that need to be sown so that we can reap the harvest that comes as a result of our plan of action.

- Take time to plan

- Check your plan often

- Be aware of your personal derailers

Examine your options and choose the best from what is available

The spirit of a man is constructed out of his choices.

Irvin D. Yalom

Choice always exists. In some circumstance this is difficult to believe, but there is always choice available to us even if the options are limited. When we accept the fact of the existence of choice, it creates a sense of possibility in our mind. When we feel cornered and find ourself in a place where it seems that we no longer have any agency, we should step back and become an observer of what is happening. What would we advise someone else to do in such a situation? Would we see choices for them that we don't see for ourself?

Ask for advice from those who have experience | We should first choose to stand back and give ourself space to get perspective on the situation and then find options. They exist; it's a matter of deciding to look for them. We can ask for advice from others who can help (though we should avoid asking for advice from those who have no experience of what we are going through. Humans seem to be programmed to give advice irrespective of whether or not they know what they are talking about). By really believing that we always have choice—and it is a hard ask sometimes—we empower ourself to become active agents in our own life.

With hindsight, can we see the options that existed?

If we think of times when we felt we had no choice, when we were at the end of our tether, overwhelmed by the weight of something we couldn't negotiate our way around, we see that we had given up on—or not recognised—the existence of choice. If we were to go through those times again, would we react in the same way? Or, with the benefit of hindsight and distance, would we see that there were other options that we hadn't noticed at the time?

In 2003, I was one hour from the top of the world, I was completely exhausted and felt as if I was in an altered state of consciousness. Unknown to me, my oxygen supply had jammed and I had developed pulmonary and cerebral oedema. I became hypoxic and lost my peripheral vision. I sat like a drunk on the south side of Mount Everest, quite happy not to move as I watched the team I was leading reach the summit. But I was weakening by the minute and my chances of dying were rapidly increasing. Even though, in my hypoxic state, I wanted nothing more than to sit there and wait for the others, an inner voice kept reminding me that if I didn't move down the mountain I would definitely die.

We always have choices

I had to make a choice: sit there and die or descend and have a chance of survival. It seems like a simple choice when it's written down on a page many years later but, at that moment, in Everest's Death Zone, it took a supreme act of will to force myself to stand up and go down the mountain. I had a choice and I chose to stand up and go down. Time was of the essence. If I waited for my team to reach me, I would have become too weak to move so I started on a crazy descent, not able to see properly and knowing I was running the risk of falling off the mountain face.

My team eventually caught up with me and helped me get back to safety. The next year, I came back and reached the summit of Mount Everest for the second time. But I learned that day that there are always

Not making a decision is also a choice

choices and sometimes we have to do the thing we don't want to do in order to survive. I also learned that doing nothing is the worst choice of all.

Actively making choices is something we decide to do; it demands effort. 'Not choosing' is also a choice. In not choosing, we abdicate from pro-actively engaging in the decision-making process and end up feeling as if we are victims of a particular situation. All our choices have consequences and, in choosing, we should be mindful of the possible consequences. Even when we decide *not* to make a choice, we are, in fact, choosing another option, and that option will also lead somewhere. It is not easy to always be thinking about what the consequences of our choices might be, but we should keep them in mind, especially when it comes to the most important things in our life.

- Practise seeing the existence of choice in all aspects of your life

- Practise making the best available choice that you can every day

- Remember that choices always have consequences

- Choosing not to act is also a choice

Opportunity is everywhere: learn how to identify it

Opportunity is everywhere. How often have we heard of someone creating something new, coming up with a fantastic new idea, or inventing a new approach to something that already works but is outdated and asked, 'Why didn't I think of that?'. The answer is that opportunity is everywhere but, unless we look for it, finding it will remain a mystery. The game of treasure hunt is a good metaphor for how we recognise and find opportunity. When we are playing treasure hunt, we know the treasure is somewhere, usually in our immediate vicinity. We have a list of clues which we listen to, read and ask about. Then we set off, eyes and ears open, looking for that which we know is somewhere around us.

It is the same with opportunity. Wherever we stand, there is opportunity around us. In Kolkata, many of the city's poorest people make a living from the Dhapa rubbish dump, spending their

Give opportunity to others when you can

days working in terrible conditions in order to earn money. Necessity drives the people who live here as they have no other income and in the infested mountains of filth they see opportunity for survival. Sometimes the opportunity we see may not be what we want, but we shouldn't doubt that it is there.

Not only do we need to be on the lookout for the opportunities that are all around us, we also need to give opportunities to others when we are in a position to do so. In our world, many people have the door shut in their face when it comes to certain types of opportunities—educational, housing, work—and it is a good act to ensure that the door is open for anyone who wants to come through it.

When your gut says it's right, go for it

There are few of us who haven't thought that an opportunity exists only to dismiss it almost immediately. This kind of sabotage is a habitual behaviour that doesn't serve us at all. Instead, when our gut tells us it's right, we should take the opportunity, develop it into an idea and make a plan.

- Believe that opportunity is everywhere

- Look, listen, be curious, ask, learn

- Look where others don't as well as in the obvious places

Time is not endless; plan yours and use it wisely

Time is the coin of your life. It is the only coin you have, and only you can determine how it will be spent. Be careful lest you let other people spend it for you.

Carl Sandburg

We are lucky to live in an era when the average life expectancy is 80 plus years. This seems like a lot of years, with plenty of time to get things right, to do what we need to do and live the life we want to lead. But in the vast scheme of things, 80 years accounts for nothing in a world that is over 4.5 billion years old. Our lifespan is barely a blip and, yet, the time we will live is all that we have and none of us know how much of it we will have.

We can fool ourself into thinking that our time will go on into some imagined forever, but the reality is different. Each day has the exact same number of hours and minutes; we can't make any day longer or shorter—even though some seem to fly and others drag—so we should do the only thing we can do and live the best life we can under whatever circumstances we find ourself.

Live your best life by managing your time well

To live our best life, we need to manage our time well; this is not about control as much as it is about teaching us perspective. If we really know how we spend our time, what we are doing and what we are getting out of it, that knowledge allows us see whether or not we are happy with how we are using our time. We won't get it back so we may as well try and do something that makes the effort worthwhile. Regretting how we spent our allocation of time is something none of us want, and now is the perfect time to start ensuring that we don't have any regrets.

A valuable exercise is to look at how we spend time over the period of a week. We should make a list for one week of everything we do and the amount of time spent on each activity, including time spent checking emails, going online and taking breaks while we

Make a time diary of your week

104

are at work. Once we have compiled a week-long 'time diary', we can study it and see if we are happy with how we spend our time and if what we are spending our time on is really what we want to be spending it on. We will learn a lot about ourself and our habits from our time diary.

- Do you allocate a specific time to a task and fulfil it within that time?

- When you are working on something do you allow distractions take your focus from it?

- Do you take too few or too many breaks?

- Do you let work spill over into your non-work time?

- How do you spend your leisure time?

- How much of your time each week is spent on important tasks and how much is spent on unimportant tasks?

When we analyse our time diary, we can decide if we are happy with how we spend our daily allocation of 24 hours, or if we can be more efficient so that we can achieve a better balance between work and leisure time. It is also important to see how productive we are. It is so easy to spend way too much time on something when the same, or similar, results could be achieved in a much shorter time-frame.

It seems to be part of the human make-up that, no matter how much time we allocate to something, that is the amount of time it will take us to do it. So we need to get the balance right and ask if the amount of time we give to specific tasks is, in fact, too much or too little. If we allocate a shorter time to complete it, would we also get it done in that time without affecting the quality of our work?

Are you happy with how you spend your time?

I learned clear lessons about efficiency on my Polar expeditions where any wasted time equalled wasted energy which could spell the end of our hopes of reaching the South Pole and, crucially, of

Balance energy input and output

surviving in such a harsh environment. Before setting off, the balance between energy, speed and time was calibrated finely. We knew exactly how long we should be moving each day, how many kilometres we should cover in that time and the energy it would take. These expeditions were run like a military operation because, if we were out in -40 degrees for any longer than we had anticipated, we were depleting our energy and resources.

We planned to walk for ten hours a day and if we didn't utilise our time properly, due to the conditions we were in we could end up adding two hours to each day pulling a sled and eating up valuable

Inefficiency can put our goals, dreams and life in jeopardy

energy. Over 60 days, this would add up to 120 hours in exposed and unforgiving conditions and could add up to ten extra days to the overall expedition. Such inefficiency would have put our lives and the success of the expedition in jeopardy.

When we become more efficient in how we spend our time, then we work and play smarter. When we apply this approach to time and how we use it, we begin to see it as a resource that is limited and that needs to be managed and spent with care and consideration. We should start managing our time so that, at the end of it, we are happy with how we spent it.

- Keep a time diary

- Become aware of how you spend your time

- See if you are happy with how you spend it

- Commit to spending more time doing what you like and less time doing what you don't like

- Prioritise your tasks daily and do the most important ones first

- Allocate a specific amount of time to complete each task and stick rigidly to that; use a clock if you need to until you learn the new habit of spending only the amount of time on a task that you know it demands

- When you are doing something—no matter what it is—give it your total focus; that way you'll get it done quicker and, most likely, better

- Identify and get rid of time-wasting habits

- Become ruthless with how you organise your day until you have learned better time-management habits, even if this involves giving up some of your favourite distractions

- Allocate time each day to exercise and get some fresh air

- Give yourself switch-off time and do something you enjoy; it's as important not to waste leisure time as it is not to waste work time

- Get as much sleep as you need, not more and not less

- Know before going to bed what you will be doing the next day; have tomorrow's diary organised in advance so that you don't waste time in the morning wondering what to do first

- Factor in time for the unexpected

- Spend as much time as possible with the people you'd like to spend more time with, especially family and friends

I have the power to:

- *Not give up*

- *Make a plan*

- *Be disciplined*

- *Make choices*

- *See opportunity everywhere*

- *Manage my time*

THE ATTRIBUTES NEEDED TO ACHIEVE GOALS

If we don't wake up in the morning with commitment in our heart to whatever it is we want to achieve, then the day ahead will be tough. We must consciously commit to our goals and put our full focus on them every day. This is not easy. It demands attributes that, if we don't already have them, we have to practise, just like apprentices, until we are skilled in them. These attributes— commitment, focus, patience, sacrifice, endurance, ruthlessness allied with compassion, and courage—aren't always easy to learn but they are worth their weight in gold and will strengthen our backbone for the adventure of life.

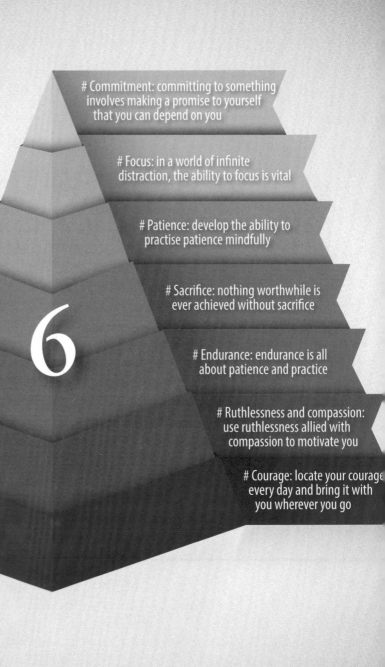

6

Commitment: committing to something involves making a promise to yourself that you can depend on you

Focus: in a world of infinite distraction, the ability to focus is vital

Patience: develop the ability to practise patience mindfully

Sacrifice: nothing worthwhile is ever achieved without sacrifice

Endurance: endurance is all about patience and practice

Ruthlessness and compassion: use ruthlessness allied with compassion to motivate you

Courage: locate your courage every day and bring it with you wherever you go

Commitment: committing to something involves making a promise to yourself that you can depend on you

Reaching our goals takes full and real commitment. Wanting to do something, or deciding that we are going to do it, isn't enough. Conscious commitment to action and sticking with the process is what takes us from intention to action to realisation. When we commit to something, we decide to direct our energy towards that goal, that project, that relationship. Our level of commitment not only shapes how we approach a project, it also affects those around us in the same way that we are impacted by their level of commitment.

> Be with people who share your goals and passion

There are few of us who haven't been on teams or in relationships where our level of commitment has not been matched. When this happens it is very difficult to maintain our own level, especially if the person spearheading the project is obviously lacking in commitment. We feel as if we are wasting our time—and we probably are—and become disillusioned. That is why it is important to ensure that we are with people who share our goals and whose commitment level matches ours.

In 2006, I decided to organise the 'Beyond Endurance' expedition where ordinary men and women would make a journey to Antarctica and South Georgia Island. The trip was to honour the achievement of Ernest Shackleton who had travelled there in an attempt to save his crew who were stranded on Elephant Island. I was also remembering other Irish Polar heroes of mine, including Tom Crean, Robert Ford, Patrick Keohane, and Tim and Mortimer McCarthy. My team and I wanted people who would challenge themselves to do something extraordinary which would demand total commitment. We put an ad in the papers that read: 'WANTED:

> Do something extraordinary

Ordinary men and women for extraordinary expedition to Antarctica. We train, you may die. Hazardous journey. Adventure guaranteed.'

I had no idea if anyone would be interested and was amazed to receive 2,500 applications. Then we faced the challenge of assessing whose commitment would bring them through the trials, tests and training needed to prepare for the journey. Two years of planning and preparation went into the trip, including 14 months of trials in Ireland and Norway, as we assessed and determined who would make the final cut. Finally, with a team of 32—the largest ever group to undertake this extreme crossing on the sub-Antarctic island—we set off on 6 November 2006.

Commitment demands time, energy, enthusiasm and belief

The commitment was a leap of faith into the unknown for our group of wannabe explorers and it was a lesson to us all as we watched their transformation from inexperienced people to hardened adventure-travellers. Initially armed only with their commitment to the journey, they struggled with the elements and their own physical limitations as they learned the outdoor skills necessary for survival in the Antarctic.

The team finally set sail for South Georgia where the traverse party battled with glaciers and Antarctic mountain ranges to successfully complete the South Georgia crossing, following in the footsteps of their heroes. This group of ordinary men and women gave themselves a massive goal and committed to the challenge of turning their dreams into reality. In doing so, they achieved more than they ever could have believed was possible.

Commitment demands our time, energy, enthusiasm and belief. If we are reluctant or doubtful, then we cannot commit, and if we cannot commit, then we are wasting our time and that of others. Being a 'warm body' is not something we should ever be. Ironically, our level of commitment does not reflect our desire for something; we may, in fact, want something very much but allow other constraints put our goals on the backburner.

- Check your level of commitment to your goals and commit to those that are most relevant to you at this time

- Do not over-extend yourself; say no if you have to—real commitment takes time

Focus: in a world of infinite distraction, the ability to focus is vital

You will never reach your destination if you stop and throw stones at every dog that barks.

Winston Churchill

When we are fully focused on something, the distractions around us recede and we are in harmony; we are doing what we need to do to get where we want to go. This state of harmony, or flow, acts almost as a buffer pushing away the many distractions that are there—like barking dogs—trying to get our attention. However, finding and maintaining our focus is not easy when there are distractions everywhere. In our online world today, we carry potential distractions with us wherever we go.

It takes a conscious committed effort to become and remain focused. When we are focused, we make progress because we are engaged; when our focus is lessened we achieve less. We might still complete the task or reach our end goal, but it takes longer and the integrity and enjoyment of the journey is challenged by distractions.

In high-altitude mountaineering, total focus is vital; you literally have to give your full attention to every step you are taking because, if you put a foot wrong, the price can be serious injury or even death. High-altitude climbers learn to focus in a number of ways and this can be applied to all areas in life.

- Choose one task and focus on that

- Make sure you are in the right environment to carry out the task—pare down what you need to do and the equipment you need to the essentials

- Ensure you are trained and skilled for whatever it is you are about to undertake; if you aren't sufficiently skilled, no amount of focus will overcome your (probably well-founded) self-doubt

- Eliminate external distracters whether they come in the form of loud and/or distracting noise; bright and/or flashing light; people who are talking to you or in any way pulling you away from your focus

We can tone down the internal distracters that continually arise in our mind by learning to observe but not engage with such thoughts and non-stop internal talk. It is impossible to stop them, but when we disengage from them, they move on and don't take our attention. In time—and especially if we practise mindfulness and meditation—the thoughts and inner talk move increasingly into the background and it becomes much easier to remain in a state of focus on whatever it is we are doing at a given time.

Use mindfulness to disengage from non-stop internal talk

We can train ourself to stay at one activity for a specific period of time by taking the necessary steps and following them. Our physical actions send a message to our brain that we are preparing for full focus and, with practice, it happens.

- Use the image and emotion of reaching your goal as a lighthouse directing you

- Don't let any internal or external voices distract you from your focus

- Focus on what you can do and not on what you can't, while all the time seeking to expand your skills and abilities

- Those with focus, discipline and motivation are most likely to achieve their goals

Patience: develop the ability to practise patience mindfully

Patience and tenacity are worth more than twice their weight of cleverness.

Thomas Henry Huxley

Patience is not only a virtue but a fantastic skill, tool, quality and friend. In today's world of instant gratification, where we want everything right now, patience doesn't get the respect it once had. However, without patience, life is much more difficult and our goals are harder to reach because, no matter how much we prepare, we will always encounter challenges that call for patience above all else.

> **Patience is not only a virtue but a fantastic skill**

Patience is a quality that high-altitude climbers and Polar explorers must develop because they constantly encounter situations where they just have to sit and wait—for better weather, for a food delivery, for assistance in the case of an accident. On extreme expeditions adventurers must learn to bow to the superior might of nature. Those who aren't patient run the risk of moving from an area of calculated risk into one of danger where the odds are increasingly stacked against them.

In 1994, when I was climbing Denali (Mount McKinley) in Alaska, we had a bad weather forecast. A number of teams ignored the warnings and continued their summit attempts. They didn't want to wait out the incoming storm because they felt that they could climb in such adverse conditions. The weather, however, beat them back. Our team, on the other hand, took the decision to sit out the storm.

For four long days we sat in our tents, trying to pass the time and hoping for a break in the weather. When it finally came, we made our summit attempt and succeeded. Those who hadn't had the patience to wait out the storm had depleted their energy and food reserves and had to retreat down the mountain even though the post-storm weather was perfect for a summit attempt.

> **Those who hadn't had patience had to descend**

In life, having patience helps us in many ways: it forces us to consider our pace and slow down if necessary. When we slow down we get a chance to look around and view the bigger picture. Patience with others teaches us about trust and compassion because, when we practise patience, we allow space for others' imperfections. We learn that we all do things at different speeds and in different ways.

We all do things at different speeds and in different ways

Patience teaches us to tolerate diversity and human uniqueness. It enables us to increase our tolerance levels—of others, of challenges, of hardship. If we learn to become truly patient then we also achieve calmness, along with the ability to persist and persevere. We are all familiar with the image of the hot-headed, impatient person who is always on the go, or the driver who breaks all the speed limits and yet doesn't really gain any time. The stop and yield signs are everywhere in life and it is up to us to choose to abide by them patiently or impatiently.

We sometimes equate impatience with progress when really it is a misuse of ours—and everyone else's—energy. There is a speed at which a car should be driven where it is at its maximum efficiency, and this is not the highest speed that the car can travel at. A car's fuel efficiency decreases once it passes its optimal speed of 88 to 96kmph. If we drive at a high speed, we waste the car's fuel. Likewise, in our life, if we 'spend' our own energy wastefully by over-exertion and unnecessary speed, we burn ourself out. We should never mistake patience and a slower pace with inefficiency or lack of productivity. If we want to maximise efficiency and progress in all areas of our life then we need patience to make a properly informed assessment of the pace needed.

There is almost always a price to be paid for being impatient and hasty. When we are impatient we come across as rude, arrogant, self-important, mistrusting and unkind. Impatience creates a barrier between us and others just as patience creates a sense of connection. When we are patient we are, by default, connecting with whatever and whoever we are patient with: we see the bigger picture and we understand what is going on. When we are impatient—rushing and speeding and wanting everything now—we lose sight of what is actually happening. When we are impatient the quality of what we are doing and of our interactions with others suffers; no one benefits from impatience and unnecessary rushing.

When we pace ourself, emotionally and physically, we reach our goals with integrity and awareness. By being patient with ourself, we tune into how we are feeling and what we are capable of. Likewise, patience with others allows us learn what it is they need to move forward.

With patience you develop:

- Compassion

- Trust

- Understanding

- Love of self and of others

- The ability to see the bigger picture

- Calmness and composure

- Perseverance

- Self-control

Sacrifice: nothing worthwhile is ever achieved without sacrifice

There is something about the word 'sacrifice' that doesn't appeal to us; it sounds hard and tough and we can almost feel the pain it implies. Its appeal is even less in a world which promises quick fixes, easy and immediate results, and click-of-the-finger magic which will make our dreams come true. The reality is that following any dream and reaching any worthwhile goal demands sacrifice. Nothing worthwhile is ever achieved easily. People famed for their 'natural' ability and genius are always at pains to point out the years of sacrifice, practice and hard work it takes to reach their goal with seemingly 'effortless' skill.

When we think about our goal, we have to ask ourself what we are willing to give up—to sacrifice—to achieve it. We need to be clear about the lifestyle, the habits and the indulgences that will act as

Nothing worthwhile is ever achieved easily

impediments to reaching our goal. When we honestly acknowledge to ourself the sacrifice involved, then we must ask if we are willing to make the necessary sacrifice. If the goal or dream is worth it, the answer will be yes. We know that what we will gain is more valuable than what we are giving up because, while sacrifice is not easy, the achievement of the goal promises to bring more than what we will have to sacrifice.

Giving up things we like, abstaining from indulgence, learning to break habitual thinking and ways of being in order to achieve something new and important in our life journey also shapes us in the process so that we change and become stronger. We learn that we have strength to do difficult things as long as we have a clear goal that is of value to us. Additionally, we discover that there are many habits that we don't want to return to. As is the case with anything we take a break from, we gain perspective and realise that taking up an old habit feels a bit like going back to somewhere we don't want to be any longer. Sacrifice clears the path for new ways of being that

Sacrifice changes us and makes us stronger

acknowledge that we are ever-evolving.

Of course, there will be parts of our old way of life that we will regret having to give up, things that we really love but which prevent us from achieving our new goal. When we miss them most we should ask ourself if we would be willing to give up our dream to have that life back again. There is always a trade-off: we sacrifice something to attain something of greater value. We should, however, heed the lesson to be learned in the mountaineer's dictum that 'achieving the summit of any mountain is not worth losing even a toe'. There are many who have lost fingers and limbs to frostbite but no mountaineer sets out to sacrifice themselves to such an extent that they are disfigured and maybe can never climb again.

For me, it was late in the day when I learned the lesson—not as a mountaineer but as a father—that too much sacrifice can be devastating. Shortly after the birth of my grandson, Jack, my son came to me. 'Dad,' he said, 'we are very proud of you but do you realise what you sacrificed to achieve your goals? You missed family events, parent-teacher meetings, weddings, funerals of close relatives, family holidays. Do you know you cannot get any of those back? Now that you have a grandchild will you consider giving more time to family?'

He was saying a truth that I had been ignoring for a long time. But I was one of the lucky ones; my family gave me another chance to rebuild a close relationship with them. It is what I cherish most in my life today above and beyond any other achievement.

- When you set yourself a new goal, be clear about what you are willing to sacrifice in order to attain it

- Do not damage yourself—mentally, physically or emotionally—by too much sacrifice

Endurance: endurance is all about patience and practice

By endurance we conquer

Ernest Shackleton's family motto

It may be coincidence that Ernest Shackleton's ship on his renowned expedition to Antarctica (1914-1917) was called *Endurance*. However, it is no coincidence that endurance was an attribute that he used every single day on the expedition and during the months of his crew's enforced exile on Elephant Island, cut off from the rest of the world and the probability of rescue. It is also telling that the name of the camp set up on an ice-floe after the crew had to abandon *Endurance* when ice crushed her hull and she started taking on water was 'Patience Camp'.

In spite of finding themselves in the bleakest of conditions, Shackleton and his men never gave up hope. They kept on fighting for survival for almost two years, always believing they would return home. They didn't give up and didn't quit. When things have gone wrong

By not quitting and by enduring, I have succeeded

for me, I have always taken great solace from the lessons learned from Shackleton and, by not quitting and by enduring, I have succeeded.

It was, in fact, when I was very young—only 14 years old—that I had my first lesson in endurance, at the North Monastery School in Cork city. I'd never had an easy time at school and was finding myself increasingly in trouble with the teachers. I was challenging their authority most of the time. After a serious incident, I knew my days there were numbered. I wanted to leave immediately but the principal, Brother Keating, wanted me to stay on until the end of term.

Endurance is not easy but it makes us stronger

He asked me if I liked school. I told him I hated it. He said that, in exchange for not expelling me or reporting my transgression to my parents, I was to tell myself every single day that I liked school. I thought this was ridiculous but, to save myself from having to face my parents' anger, I agreed. I thought the Brother was a fool. I had no intention of doing what he'd asked and thought I'd gotten off very lightly. To my surprise, every day for the remainder of the term, Brother Keating sought me out and asked me the question, 'Do you like school?'. 'Yes, I do, Brother,' I would reply. After a while, I was amazed to find that I had, in fact, started to like school for the first time ever.

The lesson I learned from this, though I didn't know it at the time, was that no matter how bad things are, if you tell yourself they are okay, then your brain starts receiving this message and you find that something you thought you couldn't succeed in becomes achievable. I have used this 'brain trick' on many occasions when I've found myself in very challenging situations and felt that my endurance was being tested.

Endure for one step more

During some of the most arduous slogs on the ice on the way to the South Pole, when I thought I couldn't take another step, I would remember what Brother Keating said to me. I'd say to myself, 'This is okay, I can do this and I am going to have great stories to tell from this experience'. Sending this message to my brain gave me the willpower to endure for one step more, and then another, until we finally reached the Pole.

It is true, however, that our life should not be endured only, but lived joyfully and fully. There are times, for all of us, when we find ourself in a place where, if we don't endure, we will lose. Endurance is not easy, but it makes us stronger and more able. When we are called on to endure something that we know needs to be gone through, then we should take just one step more, and keep doing that. If we can do that, in time, we will become the hero of our own life.

When I first set up in business, my mother gave me a verse that struck a chord and which retains its resonance, particularly at times when quitting seems the most appealing option.

> *When things go wrong, as they sometimes will,*
> *When the road you're trudging seems all uphill,*
> *When the funds are low and the debts are high*
> *Rest if you must, but don't you quit.*
> *Success is failure turned inside out -*
> *The silver tint in the clouds of doubt,*
> *And you never can tell how close you are,*
> *It might be near when it seems afar;*
> *So stick to the fight when you're hardest hit -*
> *It's when things seem worst that you must not quit.*

Ruthlessness and compassion: use ruthlessness allied with compassion to motivate you

Using ruthlessness as a tool to negotiate in life and business is no longer popular as we embrace a more compassionate, people-centred approach. Of course, we all still want to be successful, but success gained by riding roughshod over others, or deceiving them, or not caring about any pain we might cause, is not acceptable, and rightly so. There are times, however, when tough calls have to be made, in our personal life as well as our work life, in companies, on sports teams and wherever people are striving to achieve.

When it comes to making tough calls, such as dropping someone from the team, we have to be able to do it for the greater good of the goal and the rest of the team members. We cannot let one person who is no longer fulfilling their role determine the fate of the group. In situations like this, we cannot let our emotions dictate our decision-making, and this may call for the judicious use of ruthlessness to help us focus on what needs to be done for the greater good.

There are times when tough calls have to be made

A good leader—who also uses ruthlessness in an informed and intelligent manner and allied with compassion—will have all the team on board. Team members will know that the tough call is about safeguarding the goal and the wider team; they will be self-leaders and will understand the call because the leader will have communicated clearly with them. They will know that it isn't personal, although the leader will understand that pain will be felt. A good leader will have outlined the rules, goals, logistics, the standards to be met and the method by which they will be met, through proper training, support and communication.

On a number of occasions on my climbing expeditions, team members have become ill due to altitude. I knew that, ultimately, if each individual didn't make the decision themselves to retreat that I would have to do it for the safety of the team. They understood this and so did I. Fortunately, on each occasion, as self-leaders they took that decision before I, as team leader, had to. It was never easy, but all understood that being ruthless was necessary for survival.

In our personal life, when we want to get rid of old habits and learn new ways of being in the world, we can often find it very difficult to make progress and move forward. It is so much easier to stay the same, or take one step forward and two steps back. At times like this, being ruthless with ourself can help. If we are totally honest with ourself and leave nowhere to hide, then our chances of really moving

A good leader outlines the goals and provides training and support

on are better than when we take a softly-softly approach and are too easy on ourself.

At all times, however, we have to maintain compassion, for ourself and for others. Without this, ruthlessness descends into cruelty; but with compassion, judicious ruthlessness can help us find and maintain our focus at times when we feel that we are losing direction.

Courage: locate your courage every day and bring it with you wherever you go

'Fortune favours the brave.' This phrase has been in continuous use since it was first recorded in the second century BC right up to the present day. Armies, companies, families, leaders and individuals have adopted it as their motto. No one has ownership of it; it is a motto for anyone who chooses to be courageous. Courage can be described as the ability, strength of character and determination to act or stand up for something or someone in which we truly believe in the face of adversity, resistance or criticism.

Choose to be courageous

In 2008, under some of the most adverse conditions imaginable, my friend and fellow climber Pemba Gyalje Sherpa spent over two days in the Death Zone of K2, the world's second highest mountain, courageously searching for the other climbers who were lost on the mountain's upper reaches. Eleven climbers had already died and several were still missing. Most of the remaining teams had descended but Pemba stayed there, beyond the call of duty, in the attempt to save the lives of others. His courage ensured the survival of at least three other climbers who were lost. At any time, staying for so long in the Death Zone, he could have died, but he had the courage to put his life on the line for others. As a result of his actions, he was named the National Geographic Hero of the Year in 2008.

Courage comes from confidence in yourself and your belief system

We can learn to be courageous from our role models. If courageousness is not something we have already learned, then we can decide to learn it now, at this point in our life. Whatever is ahead of us, we can choose to face it with the courage of our convictions. Courage comes from confidence in ourself and our belief system. We all need to have faith in ourself, to be honest with ourself, to trust in ourself, to believe in ourself and accept that we have something to offer.

I have the power to:

- *Be patient*

- *Trust myself and others*

- *Have endurance*

- *Be compassionate*

- *Be successful*

- *Communicate clearly*

APPRENTICESHIP: A JOURNEY OF LIFELONG LEARNING

When we are engaged with our life journey, we are always apprentices in some area, learning new skills and acquiring knowledge and understanding about the world we live in. To be lifelong apprentices, we have to move out of our comfort zone and embrace the challenge that new learning brings. We make mistakes which provide us with opportunities to learn as we meet our limits and move beyond them to become more proficient in everything we do.

7

As an apprentice you are always learning and gaining knowledge

View your comfort zone not as your full-time residence but as a great place to return to

Without challenge you can't learn more

Mistakes offer the best opportunity for learning

Know your limits, challenge them and move beyond them

As an apprentice you are always learning and gaining knowledge

In my walks, every man I meet is my superior in some way, and in that I learn from him.

Ralph Waldo Emerson

As long as we keep exploring our potential, we will be apprentices to some new skill or knowledge or way of being in the world. We can simultaneously be a master in one subject and an apprentice in another. When we embrace the concept of lifelong apprenticeship, then we open ourself to being in a constant state of learning, exploring and growing in knowledge and ability. Dating from the Middle Ages, apprenticeships

> ## We can be both master and apprentice

were, for centuries, accepted and honoured periods of time—usually about seven years long—during which the apprentice learned from a master craftsman or woman all the skills of their trade.

We live in an entirely different world today where immediacy and instant gratification is the norm and patience is often in short supply. All the information we need is available at the touch of a button; surely, we think, it's just a case of downloading, reading and starting straight away. We may be able to purchase information but knowledge and skills are available only through practice, experience and repetition. In other words, it is through apprenticeship with a good teacher that we learn best.

> ## We can buy information; knowledge comes from experience

When we embrace the notion of being lifelong apprentices, we accept and honour the time needed to really learn our 'craft'. We probably won't go to live with someone in order to learn the necessary skills (although in some more traditional areas this still happens) but we will find teachers and mentors, information and expert sources that allow us to build a strong and authentic foundation. During our apprenticeship we can acquire and test our new skills, all the time building up experience and expertise.

● Be prepared to put in the time and effort needed to build up your experience and hone your skills so that you can move forward with integrity and confidence

● Learn the correct technique; a lot of energy is wasted by using the wrong one

When we see our life as a journey of learning, we open ourself to the opportunities of our personal adventure. We no longer think in terms of society-enforced 'age appropriate' learning; instead, we believe that, at any age, we can learn anything. We know that we are never too old—or too knowledgeable—to start a new learning journey.

No matter how highly developed our skills and knowledge, we can always learn something new that will add to our understanding of how the world works. We learn to see another part of the bigger picture. When we are open to lifelong learning, we can feed that hunger for knowledge by acquiring new skills, gaining new expertise and exploring some new area, even if it is not obvious how we will use this new knowledge. It all adds to our store and we will find opportunities to apply our new knowledge and skills in unexpected areas as we transfer skills learned in one area to another.

We often feel when we have completed our formal education and training and received our certificates and degrees that our learning is complete. However, new projects will always demand new learning and, as we add to our skill set, we become more proficient and efficient. We should see these times as opportunities and not as a form of drudgery. There will be times when we are in places, positions and jobs that we don't like and plan to leave as soon as we can. Even then, we can focus on what skills we can learn or perfect—even if it's patience or a sense of humour; attributes that will stand to us in life generally.

● Stay open to new people, even those you think you have nothing in common with; if you are open, you can learn something from every single person and every single situation you encounter in life

- Explore new ways of approaching familiar scenarios

- Keep trying new things until you find out what you really enjoy

The best bit of advice that I got as a young man starting out in business was to find great mentors and masters of their professions and to be an apprentice, willing to listen and learn. Since then, I have served numerous apprenticeships where I found the best teachers and mentors I could in each of the disciplines and trained to the best of my ability. As time passed, I became a better apprentice and, in turn, I became the master and, eventually, the mentor in some of the areas I specialised in.

When I was 15, I was apprenticed as a bricklayer to two of the fastest bricklayers in the country, my uncles Paddy and Donie. As a builder I served my apprenticeship under my father as well as one of Ireland's most successful developers who saw my 17-year-old drive and gave me my first big break and taught me all about the property development business. As a Polar explorer and high-altitude climber I was trained by people who gave generously of their expertise, wisdom, insights and encouragement because of my passion for adventure.

The world of writing is exciting for me because it takes me completely outside my comfort zone. I was semi-literate until I reached the age of 30. Since then, I have found great teachers because of my want and passion to express myself. I went into film production in my fifties and again connected with people who believed in my vision. The first production I worked on became an international award-winning film.

> Seek out the best people you can find and ask for their help

To be the best that we can be in whatever we want to do, we should seek out the best and most experienced people we can find and ask for their help. The greatest compliment we can give any teacher is to be passionate, enthusiastic apprentices who are eager to learn. In this way we become part of their legacy.

View your comfort zone not as your full-time residence but as a great place to return to

There isn't one among us who doesn't like to feel comfortable, to occupy that space where we are most consistently at ease, with little or no stress. Here, we can rest, secure in our comfort zone and the familiarity of our routine. Our comfort zone can stretch right across every area of our life—personal, work and social. We know what we like; we know what we are comfortable doing and the people in whose company we are most relaxed.

Within our comfort zone, we live in a challenge-neutral area where our stress levels are low and where our regular routine provides us

To achieve we have to move beyond our comfort zone

with a degree of happiness and ease. The advantages of the comfort zone are many and valuable: security, little stress or risk, acceptance by those around us. The comfort zone is one where steady, dependable performance can be expected. However, if we keep setting goals within our comfort zone we will never test our ability to reach our full potential.

In 1908, psychologists Robert M. Yerkes and John Dillingham Dodson carried out experiments whose results point to a relationship between performance and physiological and mental arousal. The Yerkes-Dodson Law states that performance is improved with increased arousal, but only up to a certain point, after which excessive arousal diminishes performance. Within our comfort zone, our performance is steady but not at its peak. In order to achieve peak performance, we have to move beyond our comfort zone. Once we

We relax in our comfort zone

are beyond this zone, we start to feel anxiety and raised stress levels which help enhance our performance.

We often hear actors say that no matter how experienced and admired they are, they still get nervous before coming onto the stage. They always add that if they didn't experience such nervousness, they believe it would be time for them to quit. This 'nervousness' reflects an engagement with the desire to give an optimal performance and to do one's best. The right amount of stress or nervousness is needed; too much and we can become frozen and incapable of performing at all.

Train yourself to perform optimally

When we accept that our comfort zone is a good place for us to rest and relax but not a good place to remain all of the time, we can train ourself to move beyond that zone into a space of higher anxiety where performance is optimised. This can be done in simple ways.

- Change your daily routine; this can be as simple as taking a different route to work

- Talk to someone you would normally not engage with

- Eat food you think you hate but have, in fact, never tried

- Learn a new skill for which you have no natural aptitude

In that place beyond our comfort zone, where we are experiencing higher anxiety levels and performing at a higher level, we are on a learning curve that takes us to our limits and challenges us to go beyond them as we learn. We also gain skills that are beneficial when adversity and challenge enter our life. Beyond our comfort zone we use mental muscles which can get flabby and weak when left unexercised. We must remember, though,

We use mental muscles which can get flabby if unused

not to push ourself too far, too fast. By adopting a gradual approach, we can learn that the world beyond our comfort zone is a fascinating place in which we can make a significant contribution.

Without challenge you can't learn more

If you don't challenge yourself, you will never realise what you can become.

Anonymous

What is it that drives us to challenge ourself to succeed? To push ourself just that bit further? To be the best we can be? During over 30 years of exploration around the world, I have met people from every walk of life and many countries, including Stone Age tribes in West Papua New Guinea, and I have seen that the desire to challenge oneself is common to all nations and races. We all want to be winners and to be part of a winning team. It is part of human nature to challenge ourself and to strive to be the best that we can be. We need challenge just like we need food and, without it, we stagnate into dullness and mediocrity.

We feel great when we rise to a challenge

There is a great feeling of satisfaction when we rise to a challenge and succeed. It doesn't matter what the challenge is; the important thing is to engage with something unknown or difficult and learn how to handle and master the task. We do this as children every day when we learn, literally, to find our feet in the world. Our parents and educators teach us about challenge through play and sport. We all know what it is like to progress from four-piece to ten-piece jigsaws and on and on until we can do 1,000-piece jigsaws. All the time we are being challenged to learn more, to push ourself, to tap into our capability and to use our skills.

Athletes challenge themselves constantly; if they didn't they would never win or continue winning. They reach a personal best, and then they set a new challenge to surpass that. By setting new challenges,

Tap into your ability

they learn how to remain focused and disciplined despite previous success.

As adults, we also like to be challenged but we often forget this in the busyness of life. When we learn a skill and are good at what we do it is tempting to think, 'That's it, I can keep doing this and the wheels will keep turning'. Most likely they will keep turning but they won't go any faster and, over time, they will probably go slower. When we avoid new challenges, we become complacent, stale and uncreative. If we do the same thing, day after day—even if we are really good at it—we lose proficiency over time because we lose focus. New challenges keep our focus sharp and help us to tap into our creativity as we seek to complete the 'jigsaws' of adult challenges. Taking on something new helps nourish our creative side; it encourages us to think outside the box and to expand our experience of life.

> When we avoid new challenges, we become complacent, stale and uncreative

In my early years, when I was at the top of my game in property development, I had a great team of directors, managers and workers. They had become part of my team because of my vision, focus, direction and strategy. As a leader, I was driven to succeed and grow the business, and my team bought into the challenge of being the best that we could be. After I had achieved my goals, I became complacent. I failed to realise that my team also had personal and professional goals, and wanted and needed to be further challenged.

I was too controlling and should have handed over the reins to those who wanted to drive the business further. This oversight came at a high price; my team's enthusiasm and trust in me crumbled when I overtraded and lost focus. That, coupled with an economic recession, ensured the eventual collapse of my business.

I learned my lesson and, for over 20 years now, I spend many months each year travelling the world, seeking out challenges that stimulate me and the teams I work with. I understand that people constantly need new challenges and new goals. Most people—whether or not they are aware of it—aspire to lead more challenge-based lives. To fully participate in the adventure that is our life, we should embrace challenge and travel to the places it brings us.

- Challenge allows you to succeed
- Challenge helps you to learn
- Challenge keeps your mind alert

● Challenge helps you focus on success

● Succeeding at challenges, no matter what they are, helps build self-esteem and confidence

Mistakes offer the best opportunity for learning

A life spent making mistakes is not only more honourable, but more useful, than a life spent doing nothing.

George Bernard Shaw

Can any one of us honestly say there has been a day in our life where we haven't made a mistake, big or small? In fact, most of us are happy to get through 24 hours having made only small mistakes whose reverberations aren't too far-reaching. I have failed more often than I have succeeded throughout my life. I have, however, learned more from my mistakes and failures that I ever learned from my successes. Now, when I have a new goal or project, I look at my past mistakes and those of others and use what I learn from them to formulate new and better plans.

● Accept that everybody makes mistakes and there is no point in beating yourself up when you make one; making mistakes is a natural part of living and learning

● Do your best to ensure that you don't make the same mistake time and time again; you are not addressing an underlying issue if this happens

- Don't look for someone else to blame when you make a mistake; blaming is a waste of time and energy and doesn't make you any friends

- Learn from your mistakes

- Try to learn from the mistakes of others, especially if you find yourself in a similar position

- Forgive yourself and keep moving in the direction of your goal

- Remember that, no matter how skilled or experienced you are, you are never, ever beyond making a mistake

Know your limits, challenge them and move beyond them

Once we accept our limits, we go beyond them.
Albert Einstein

In life, we are very focused on learning about the world around us—about how it works and what our place is in it—and we often neglect to engage in learning about ourself. We lack self-knowledge and make assumptions about what we can and cannot do based on what others tell us and on what we tell ourself without truly examining what it is we are capable of doing. In gaining self-knowledge it is very important that we find, know, accept and then reach beyond our limits. We need to know the extent of our skills and knowledge, of our strengths and weaknesses. We need to know how confident we are and how strong our self-belief is.

Find, know, accept and reach beyond your limits

It is only when we know our limits that we can move beyond them, and we should always be challenging ourself to move beyond our current limits. If, for example, we are aiming to get fit, we should

We all have limitations; there isn't one of us who can do everything

challenge ourself to just within our limits when we are doing a workout. Once we know what that limit is, then we can keep on the right side of not over-extending ourself. At the same time, we can push ourself a bit more each time we work out, challenging

ourself to stay at the exercise for just a little longer. By recognising our limits and challenging ourself to move beyond them, step by step, we make progress and advance towards a bigger goal. When we move beyond earlier limits, it is a moment to mark and celebrate.

It is important, however, to respect our limits, even while always seeking to expand them and learn more. If a climber climbs beyond their limits, then they move into the danger zone. This applies in all areas of life; if we move beyond our limits without giving ourself proper time to prepare and train for what lies ahead, then we put ourself in situations where we are more likely to fail and get injured, physically or emotionally. On many occasions in my early business life, I pushed beyond the limits of my knowledge and went on pure gut reaction. I made the wrong choices and lost much on the gambles I took. I learned from these mistakes and brought those lessons into my adventure life and, later, back into my business dealings.

We all have limitations; there isn't one of us who can do everything and this is why we need other people around us. In areas where our limits are significant, then we need to accept that we need the help of others and to know that somebody has our back. With those people, we can form good teams; we can observe and learn while focusing on the areas where our skills are best.

My friend, the elite Russian Kazakh mountaineer, Anatoli Boukreev, did just this in 1997 when he was hired to lead a team on Mount Everest. His climbing skills were superb but he recognised that he didn't have an easy-going personality. He hired team members whose experience he admired and whose personalities would counter the aspects of his own which he saw as negative. Boukreev was honest in his assessment of his own limits and did what he needed to do to ensure those limits didn't harm the team's chance of achieving their goal.

Sometimes we don't want to test our limits because we fear how little we know, but if we don't face up to what they are we never move beyond them; we never expand our knowledge or learn what we need to move forward confidently.

- Get over any fear you may have of finding out what your limits are

- Be honest in your assessment of your limits

- Be compassionate with yourself in your assessment

We all have limits in every area of life and, in fact, our limits in any one area can change over our lifetime; they are not fixed—at different times in our life there are certain things we can do well. We need to be aware of this and adapt as necessary. Age is one thing that affects what we can and can't do and when we find that we have to give up on something we want to do, or have always done, there is no need to despair. We just adjust and re-set our goals; we familiarise ourself with our new limits and move beyond them.

I have the power to:

- Learn new skills

- Move outside my comfort zone

- Relax and enjoy life

- Learn from my mistakes

- Forgive myself

- Reach my limits and move beyond them

KEEP YOUR MIND AND BODY FIT FOR YOUR LIFE

We give ourself the greatest possible chance in life when we look after our mind and body to the best of our ability. Our mental and physical health exist on a continuum and we should check in daily on both to see how we are feeling and if we need to take any steps to safeguard either, just as we would do with our car. To maintain good general physical health, a balanced diet, regular exercise and sufficient rest are basic necessities.

For good mental health, we need to control what we 'feed' our mind. Having good people in our life, along with strong support networks and a tribe to which we belong, is a vital support for good mental health. Knowing what we want and what we stand for, and having the courage to say it also helps keep us strong mentally. Our mental and physical health are intertwined and co-dependent and tending both carefully keeps us strong.

8

Mind your mental and physical health

Be ethical and know what you stand for

Good support networks allow you to flourish

Mind your mental and physical health

When we hear the phrase, 'Your health is your wealth', we instinctively think of our physical health. But we should also think of our mental health because it is as important as our physical health and each impacts on the other. We automatically check in with our physical body: we are aware of where we feel pain, if there are aches anywhere, if we need to take a tablet or a hot bath or to call a doctor. We monitor our physical health and take the decision to act—or not to act—depending on how we are feeling.

We are surrounded by information on how to keep healthy, and most areas have a choice of general practitioners for us to attend when we need to. This

The South Pole trek was equivalent to 120 marathons

is good and, in fact, we need to be even more proactive regarding our physical health. Prevention is better than cure and by monitoring and checking in with our physical health on a regular basis, we will be both healthier and wealthier as a society, as health costs are among the highest for any government.

Before setting off on expedition, adventurers have to check in with their physical body. We have to ensure that we have trained sufficiently for the challenge ahead; that we have learned all the necessary skills and that our body is in good working order. As adventurers, our body is our vehicle and we do all that we possibly can to make sure that we are expedition-fit.

When I was training with my team for our Antarctic expedition to the South Pole, we wanted the best advice possible on how to prepare for the conditions ahead. We consulted Professor Phil Jakeman of the Elite Athletes Programme at the University of Limerick. He found that we would be expending the same amount of energy daily on the ice in Antarctica as was required to complete two marathons a day. He explained that, in terms of endurance, over our 60-day expedition, there was no real difference

I ate up to 9,600 calories daily

between what we were doing and undertaking a Tour de France cycle or 120 marathons. Because of that, we needed to learn how to consume between 6,500 and 9,600 calories daily to provide enough energy for each day.

With Professor Jakeman's advice, we put a programme in place to ensure our bodies were ready for the challenge. We trained by pulling up to three tractor tyres up a hill for approximately 14km every day, for a year and a half. Six weeks before going to Antarctica, my team became the first Irish team to do a 660km unsupported crossing of Greenland; about four months before that we completed a 330km expedition in Norway. It was all part of getting ourselves both physically and mentally fit for the challenge ahead which would include months of isolation.

Our bodies serve us better when fit

Just as an adventurer prepares for the challenges ahead, we should also ensure that we are physically fit for the adventure of life. It makes sense that the fitter we are and the more we look after our body, the better it will serve us in times of both illness and health.

For the adventurer, mental health is as important as physical health. Some expeditions are so tough that, long after the body is screaming to give up and stop, only the strength of the mind can power us over the finish line. When an objective danger, such as an unpredicted avalanche, occurs, we are physically powerless and it is only our mental strength that allows us deal with the fear and trauma that comes with such extreme situations.

Our mental health exists on a continuum, just as our physical health does. Some days we feel fine and other days not so fine. When we

Sometimes only your mind will get you over the line

don't feel good mentally we may not talk about it at home or at work in the way we'd mention having a headache or a sore throat. There is still a silence around mental health, the legacy of a time when anyone who didn't 'fit in' was locked away. Society is, generally, more open now but we still have a long way to go. We still want to 'fit in' and, because of that—and despite the great work being done by many organisations and individuals—we suffer in silence, not realising that everyone around us experiences the same thing to a greater or lesser degree at some point.

Our general mental health is not something fixed and static; like our body, our mind is 'alive' to all that is happening internally and externally and constantly reacting and adapting. We need to be watchful and conscious of taking care of our mind. Just as we try not to eat foods that make us ill, or undertake activities that might damage our body, we should also avoid doing and absorbing stuff that makes us ill mentally and drives us towards the extreme ends of the mental health continuum.

Our self-talk can be toxic to our mental health

Among the most powerful influencers on our mental health are the stories we tell ourself and that society tells us about ourself. We need stories and narratives to make sense of the world but we also need to be able to step back from the stories we tell ourself about ourself and others if they are making us ill.

Our self-talk can be more toxic to our mental health than anything anyone else says to us. The voice in our head that never seems to stop can be our greatest enemy if we don't engage with it and change its narrative. We start that journey towards engagement with healthy self-talk by accepting that we all have conversations going on in our head all the time. In fact, research shows that our mind is in the present moment for only 5% of any day; the rest of the time we are in the past (rewriting it) or in the future (imagining and scripting it).

We can feel trapped in our own life, ground down by the weight of the person we feel we should be. We don't know how to escape the narrative that we and society have created for us. We know who we have been, we know who we are expected to be, but it can feel like a trap and we may no longer want to be that person. Life is changing and we want to change with it. But, for a multitude of reasons, this is not easy. We wear a 'coping face'. When asked how we are, we reply 'Fine' or 'OK' when we are anything but. We want to break out of who we have been—like a butterfly emerging from a chrysalis—into our new self but we feel

We can change the stories we tell ourselves

frightened, guilty or ashamed and become caught in a world where mental ill health snaps at the edges of our mind.

But the stories that we live our life by can be changed; we can break free of them and create new stories. This is what the modern-day adventurer does. After the natural world has been fully explored, the landscape that remains to be explored is that of the human mind. The more knowledge and information we get, the more we move towards understanding what goes on in our mind and how we can engage with it so that it doesn't overwhelm us. We are advised that moderation in all is good for the physical body, and it is also good for the mind—how we nurture and keep our mind 'fit' is as important as how we do the same for our body.

To keep your mind in good health:

- Have a plan

- Have time for working each day

- Have time for play each day

- Find out what well you can draw on for spiritual sustenance, whether it is music, literature, religion, climbing, running or practising yoga; whatever your 'well' is, you'll know it when you find it and if you haven't found it yet, keep looking

- Connect with people in a real way; no matter how simple the exchange, the connection should be authentic

- Eat well and exercise daily (good for the body and for the mind)

- Be honest with yourself about what you want and don't want

The single most important lesson, however, is to learn that we are not our thoughts. They come and then they go. Our mental health continuum is often tipped out of balance when we attach too much importance to our thoughts and let them define us and shape how we see the world. We live in a world that is obsessed with labelling, with saying 'She is this' and 'He is that'. This is a very constricting way of viewing life and we are both the victims and the perpetrators of labelling.

When we become more aware of how our mind works, we become more mindful. With this comes detachment from our thoughts, self-talk and labelling. The activity doesn't stop; it's just that we stop investing energy in it. We learn that the thoughts in our head are like clouds passing through the sky; they will move on, immediately, soon or eventually, and be replaced by new thoughts.

Observe what is going on in your head

By practising mindfulness—the non-judgemental awareness of our thoughts and emotions—we become more observant of what is going on inside our head. We listen to the inner voice, we are aware of the labelling and the stories that it is telling, but we create a distance between ourself and it, knowing that not only is the talk *not* who we are, but that there will be a whole other conversation going on in our head moments from now.

- Consciously practise detaching from your thoughts, whatever they are

- Be in nature

- Take time out to do nothing

- Observe your breath

- Accept that everything in life is impermanent and ever-changing

These practices are like rituals that create space and it is in that space that understanding and perspective grow. Just before setting off from Base Camp to climb in the Himalaya, the Sherpa perform the puja prayer ritual, asking the gods to keep the climbers safe. In the busyness of preparing for a major climb, the puja allows everyone to be still and mindful. It allows space for awareness of the connectivity between those

Rituals remind us we are not in control

taking part in the climb, their connection with the mountain they are about the climb and the natural world that they hope will look kindly on them. Such rituals remind us that we are not in control and that we don't have to waste energy trying to be.

- Get out of your head and into your instinct for trust and intuition

- Communicate with others about how you are feeling, just as you do when it comes to physical health issues

- Be honest with yourself

- Find professional help if you need it

- Sit with your feelings; they will pass

- Avoid isolating yourself from your family, friends and community; everybody needs to belong to some tribe

It is important that we get both our physical and mental health in order for the challenges of life. We need to have both in balance to give ourself the best possible chance of having a good life. If we don't balance our health, we become susceptible to burnout and depression. By looking after our physical and mental health, we ensure that our mind and body are functioning in harmony and allowing us live our best life.

Be ethical and know what you stand for

Broadly speaking, we are defined—and define others—by where we come from, what level of education we have attained, what we work at, where we live and what social group we belong to. We are all conscious of the measurement tools that we use to order the world and our place, and that of others, in it. But there is something much more personal that defines us and how we journey through our life and that is the belief system by which we live. Despite this, we tend to spend more time investing in our outer façade than in identifying what it is we truly believe and the code by which we want to live.

Everyone—individuals, families, communities, teams, companies—should have a clear code of ethics that serves as a behaviour guide. We can develop a code of ethics at any time in our life and, once we have one, we can re-visit it and adapt it as our life progresses and changes. The basis of our code is informed by what we believe is morally good and bad, right and wrong.

A code of ethics should reflect:

- What you believe to be right and what you believe to be wrong

- The rules of behaviour by which you will live your life

- The principles by which you want to live your life

- Your sense of responsibility to yourself, your family, social group and wider society

- Rules that allow you to protect and maintain your integrity

When we are clear on what we stand for and have a code to guide us, we are able to live more efficiently and confidently. Likewise, in teams and in the workplace, having a well-formulated code of ethics is hugely beneficial.

- It serves as a benchmark or guide for workers regarding what is and isn't acceptable within the group

- It promotes better communication when queries or problems arise

- It promotes consistency in standards and behaviour

- It helps build trust and loyalty

As individuals, teams or companies, once we have identified our values and developed a code of ethics, we need to apply them and behave in a manner that is consistent with them. If our actions are inconsistent with our own core values in order to succeed, then there is a very high price to be paid, even if we are not found out. In the world of adventure, there is constant talk around ethical climbing and adventuring. There is not always agreement between different teams on what is the most ethical way to approach a climb or an expedition, but there should always be clear agreement *within* a team on its shared code. If success is achieved in a manner that compromises our integrity or beliefs, then that success is forever tainted, both privately and publicly.

If we compromise our integrity, our success is tainted

In mountaineering, teams have different rules about helping others, particularly on high-altitude mountains. I saw this at first hand when I was climbing Aconcagua in Argentina. My climbing partner and I had just reached the peak of the mountain when we saw an American climber staggering towards us, struggling for breath and suffering badly from altitude sickness. My partner looked at me and I knew we were thinking the same thing. We had met the American earlier on the mountain, and although he wasn't part of our expedition, we felt a responsibility to ensure his safe return. Even if we hadn't known him at all, we would have come to the aid of a fellow climber. Altitude sickness can happen to anybody and I'd like to think that my fellow climbers would help me if I was suffering.

As we made our descent, the man's condition worsened until he was stumbling like a drunken man. Blizzard conditions set in and eventually it was necessary to split our group. I set off down the mountain to try and raise a rescue. Along the way I encountered other climbers, some of whom were willing to help and some who were not. The latter had a different code of practice in relation to helping people on the mountain as it would adversely affect their summit attempt. Such a code didn't sit easy with me but I understood it.

People have different codes of conduct

With extra help and resources, we constructed a makeshift sled. We had to spend another night on the mountain and finally made it down safely. Many years later I found myself suffering from oedema on Mount Everest and was, in turn, grateful for the care and attention I received from my fellow mountaineers.

● Know what you stand for

● Identify your values and belief system

● Develop a code of ethics

● Put it into practice

Good support networks allow you to flourish

Every great athlete, artist and aspiring being has a great team to help them flourish and succeed—personally and professionally. Even the so-called 'solo star' has a strong supporting cast helping them shine, thrive and take flight.

Rasheed Ogunlaru

There is very little that we can accomplish alone; in fact, there is very little that we want to accomplish alone; a shared burden is a burden halved and a shared joy is a joy doubled. There may be certain journeys that are more personal and where we have to—or want to—travel alone for certain parts, but the reality is that, even on these journeys, somebody somewhere along the route will give us help and support.

No matter what we do in life, having a support network is vitally important. This network can be made up of some or all of the following: family, friends, neighbours, our wider community, colleagues, advisors, teachers and mentors. Our networks are like life sources from which we draw what we need—energy, encouragement, refuge or support. It is a two-way street and, in a healthy network, we will give as much as we take over the lifetime of the network.

We can draw on our different networks for our different needs; one network cannot meet all our needs or share all our interests and therefore it is important to always be building new networks as well as expanding existing ones. Families provide very specific support and love, but we often have to build another network to find like-minded people when it comes to certain interests or projects we are undertaking. We should consciously build our networks all the time while being aware that the aim is not to fill our life and contacts list with endless names and numbers but, rather, to create a support system that is mutually beneficial, caring and supportive.

> **There is very little that we can accomplish alone**

When we are dreaming about new goals, we need like-minded people with whom to talk and share our ideas, people who are on a similar journey or someone who has already taken that route and can act as an advisor or mentor to us. Such a network allows us to explore the limits of what is possible, whereas discussing the same idea with a family member might not be met with such enthusiasm. Families often tend to be more cautious and risk-averse in relation to those closest to them.

> **Create support systems that are mutually supportive**

We need the support of our friends as much as, if not more than, the support of our families. The love, loyalty and support of good friends are priceless and when we make good ones we should work hard to keep those friendships healthy and flourishing. We should listen to and respect the opinions of our friends, but we shouldn't allow them to curtail our dreams—in the same way that we shouldn't try to curtail theirs. Friends can sometimes be resentful if we appear to be moving away from them and finding another group or tribe. It's important to be aware of this and not to become tied to a version of ourself that our friends like but which we have outgrown.

- Cultivate strong, healthy friendships

- Assess how you feel when you are with your friends

- Spend time with those whose energy is good

- Support those who may be going through a tough time but ensure their energy doesn't pull you down; do what you need to counter that without giving up on them

Beyond our immediate family, friends and community, we can look to other resources—locally and globally—to build our networks. We should never be afraid or ashamed to ask for help or advice. People generally are flattered when they are asked for their support. No matter what we need, there are advisors, teachers and mentors all around us whose knowledge and expertise we can tap into.

When we convey our passion to those who know more than we do, they connect with that passion which they recognise from their own journey of exploration. We should also be on the lookout for good mentors from whom we can learn by hearing their stories and heeding their advice. Good mentors can guide us when we need guiding and show us the path when we lose our way.

- Don't be afraid to make connections with experts before undertaking a big project or starting something new

- Have your skills assessed by an expert if you have doubts about them

- Develop a 'buddy' system with an expert who has your back at all times

Encouragement is very important; if we grew up without people to encourage and motivate us to be the best that we can be, then we need to find positive influences elsewhere. We may also need to move away from certain people (even family and close friends) as we enter a space of positivity, especially if some of those close to us are habitual naysayers. This doesn't necessitate cutting ties fully, but we need to build on a foundation of self-belief and positivity. Until that foundation

Don't ever be ashamed to ask for help when you need it

is strong enough, we may need to distance ourself from certain people or protect ourself from them in some way. We may feel bad about this, guilty even, but we should not allow this hold us back or stop us exploring the limits of who we can become.

We also need to assess the energy we are giving out and absorbing from the people in our life. It is very helpful to look at the people we meet on a daily basis and assess our interaction with them.

- What is the general tone and focus of your conversations?

- Is it positive or negative, expansive or contracted?

- Is there a feeling of possibility, curiosity and joy in your interactions or the opposite?

Everyone's energy is contagious: we feed off the energy of those we meet, and our energy is in some way affected by each encounter. A popular categorisation of people is as 'drains' or 'radiators'. While it is best generally to avoid either/or categorisation, this one is handy as a method of checking the effect people's energy is having on us. It is also useful for checking in on the energy we are giving out. When our mental energy dips, or when we see the warning signs that we are moving in that direction, we should take action and make a conscious effort to find positive energy to help us adjust our balance. We can make a mental note of the things and people that normally lift us up and consciously engage with these 'lifters' when we are down.

When we find people who inspire us, we should try and bring them into our life in a meaningful way—whether they are people we meet, writers whose work fires up our mind, or musicians whose music moves us in a positive way. On our journey of exploration, we ought to remember the words of Winston Churchill: 'A pessimist sees the difficulty in every opportunity; an optimist sees the opportunity in every difficulty.'

The kind of energy you need to help you flourish will convey:

- Optimism

- Realism

- Hope

- Independence

- Compassion

- Humour

I have the power to:

- *Look after my mental and physical health*

- *Control my self-talk*

- *Be ethical, honest and fair*

- *Accept love, loyalty and support*

- *Be positive*

- *Be grateful*

HOW TO
BECOME EFFICIENT

Rules, efficiency, discipline and speed are important for progress in all areas of life. Humans have been making and breaking rules since the beginning of time; we need them, but we also need to change them when they no longer serve us. When we know what the rules are and what their purpose is, then we can test them. If they are still relevant, we should keep them. If they are outdated we should have the courage to challenge and change them.

There are many distractions that eat away at our efficiency and that we need to eliminate from our life. Travelling lightly and minimising baggage—physical and emotional—allows us the freedom to move without unnecessary burdens. When we learn to cast off the stuff that is weighing us down, we can focus more on the important things. More than anything else, clear and effective communication is vital to facilitate efficiency in everything we do. We should check and double check that what we are communicating is clear to others and that we understand what is being communicated to us.

9

Rules: break them if they are not working and make better ones

#Travel light and carry only what you need

Efficiency is a key attribute for success

Communicate clearly to understand and to be understood

Rules: break them if they are not working and make better ones

From our earliest years, human beings make rules. Watch any group of children at play; if they make up a game themselves, the first thing they do is create a set of rules. Every interaction we have with another person, group or organisation has rules, either written or unwritten. We make rules to create order, structure and safety, be that physical, emotional or financial security. When we enter into a relationship with another person, we learn the rules of engagement and there is an assumption that we will play by the rules, indicating a level of trust and commitment around whatever is being undertaken.

> **We make rules to create order, structure and safety**

Protection is one of the main priorities of those who make rules. They want to protect the individual, the group and the organisation, though not necessarily in that order. When the reasoning behind a rule is obvious, most people are happy to sign up for it, but when we don't understand rules—or the reason for their existence isn't obvious—we are much more likely to break them, irrespective of the consequences.

You may ask:

- Why does this rule exist?

- What will happen if this rule is broken?

- Is there a better rule that isn't as constrictive and that will better serve you or the group?

Rules should be regularly evaluated to check their continued relevance. If we don't change or adapt rules, then progress is stymied. Before we challenge the rules, we need to be clear on what the consequences are and what we will replace them with.

● Rules should be there to protect people

● Everyone should understand why the rule exists

● When rules are outdated, they need to be updated

Travel light and carry only what you need

One of the most important tasks to do before setting off on expedition is to go through in minute detail every single thing that we will bring with us for the adventure ahead. We make a list of exactly what we need for the coming months—every piece of food, items of clothing, medical necessities and tents for sleeping in. We also allow ourself one or two 'comfort' items, maybe a book or small music player; such items are as vital as food during times of long, hard slog in harsh conditions.

Everything is weighed and packed and when we put it on our back we see how well we can carry the weight. Such exercises hone our instinct for what is necessary for survival and basic comfort. We learn the advantages of travelling light, not just on the mountains and in Polar regions, but also in life.

When we repeatedly refine what we need for a journey, it forces us to assess what is really important. We ask if we are packing something just because we own it and feel we should use it? Because it gives us comfort? Because it makes us look good? Adventurers learn to 'travel light'; to identify what is needed to get where we want to go and to leave behind the excess that will weigh us down and, in extreme situations, act as a possible threat to our survival.

Travelling light forces us to assess what we need

When we bring these habits to our daily and business life, we see all the clutter that we have accumulated, all the stuff that is weighing us down and is not of any real use. In a consumer-driven culture it is easy to keep buying new things and much harder to stop. But having lots of stuff and continuing to spend our money on more stuff makes it difficult to travel lightly. It's not just the space that stuff takes up; it is the commitment it demands. If we have stuff we need to take care of it, insure it, have it serviced and get others to check on it when we are away. Despite all that effort on maintenance, whether we like it or not, possessions don't actually make us happy or help us lead a content life.

When we de-clutter, our physical and mental spaces open up

When we step back and look objectively at all the possessions we have, we begin to learn what is really important and what is of use for our life journey. Many of us have too many clothes, most of which we never wear; too many gadgets that perform similar functions; things for rainy days that we don't even remember when the rainy days come. We have aspirational stuff that we purchased after we'd bought into an image of ourself that was never real. We have debt for things we no longer want and we have property and modes of transport that we don't need because there are only 24 hours in any one day and we can't get around to them all, and we don't really want to anyhow.

What we own and our relationship with it impacts on how we live and how we think about ourself. When our life is cluttered with things we don't need, we become weighed down and our ability to move freely and lightly is impaired. When we decide to de-clutter, we find our physical and mental spaces open up. It's like clearing a path in a jungle—we make way to move forward, unshackled by stuff that is weighing us down and holding us back.

One of the silver linings in my going broke in my late twenties was that it changed my whole way of thinking. By the time I lost my businesses, I was burnt out. I had been driven by materi-

Going broke changed my whole way of thinking

alistic success; I wanted to accumulate more financial wealth and keep up with the Joneses by having a big house and car. I was willing to work all hours and do whatever was necessary to ensure that I stayed at the top of my particular game.

After my world came crashing down around my head, I was lost. I—initially reluctantly—took up mountain climbing and soon found myself on a trip to Nepal, on my first trip to the Himalaya. However,

Create good where possible and shun negativity

I wasn't going there just to climb; I also, naively perhaps, felt this was a place where I would clear my head. Instead of 'finding myself', however, I was confused and challenged by the people I met, particularly in the towns and villages high up in the mountains. They had very little materially but had an amazing outlook on life. I learnt from them the philosophy of Buddhism.

The inspirational and wise monks from Tengboche monastery, high in the Khumbu valley near Mount Everest, willingly gave their time and energy to a lost and confused soul. They taught me that life lived simply allows us to live well. They also taught the lesson that we should be kind, grateful, mindful of others and their suffering; that we should create good where possible and shun negativity, resentfulness and hatred. I learned that we should use our talents to be the best that we can be; to get back up when we get knocked down; to have pride but not to be egotistical.

Instead of re-finding my old self, I identified a new me. I discovered a whole new way of thinking about life. I became a kinder, more realistic person who realised that material success is but one form of success, and nowhere near the most important. The lessons I learned that year in the Himalaya have stayed with me and remain my guiding principles.

With less stuff, we feel freer and we are freer. This can be a challenging concept in a world where we are encouraged to define people by what they own. It's pretty radical to consider that there is more freedom and greater authenticity to be found in owning only what we need, and in getting rid of things we thought we wanted, or that someone else said we should have. We over-identify with stuff that we own and it is only by getting rid of it that we can encounter our real self.

The benefits of travelling light are:

- You learn to prioritise

- When you are honest about what you need and want to keep in your life, you come to know yourself better

- You consume less and are a better friend to the environment

- You find space in your life to explore more easily and with greater freedom

- You use your time better because you don't have to worry about taking care of stuff

- You have more time for yourself, for family and for friends

A de-cluttered life is not a sterile environment; on the contrary, we should always aim to have the best of what we need and to prioritise quality over quantity in every aspect of our life. An adventurer can only bring a small amount of clothing with them but we should make sure it is the best quality we can buy for the expedition ahead.

Another advantage of travelling light is that we are better positioned

Always prioritise quality over quantity

to react to changing conditions. The more stuff we have, the more emotional and financial commitments we develop. Then, when things change in our life, the more difficult it is for us to react efficiently and effectively. Those of us who are travelling light and not carrying extra weight are much better positioned to adapt well to change and the unexpected.

I remember sitting patiently with my team in Resolute in the North West Passage in Canada, waiting for nearly three weeks for a weather window so that we could commence our expedition to the North Pole. We used the time to examine every single piece of equipment we had with us. The less weight we carried, the better able to move we would be. We shaved matchsticks and shoelaces to reduce our burden, even if only by a few grams, for the mission ahead. We kept refining, down to the

The less weight we had, the better

tiniest item, what we projected we needed for the 60-day expedition. We were hyper-aware of making a miscalculation because leaving ourself short of something was potentially fatal.

Experiences such as this really honed my awareness of the need to find the balance between what we really need and what we carry that slows us down and becomes a burden.

- Own only what you need and what you truly want

- Get rid of stuff that you don't use, have never used and will never use

- Let 'quality over quantity' be your motto

- Use your wealth wisely and, where possible, reach out to those who need a helping hand

Efficiency is a key attribute for success

Efficiency, discipline and speed are key requisites for every expedition. Without them, goals are rarely achieved on high mountains or in the Polar regions. If explorers don't practise efficiency in everything that we do, calculated risks turn into real dangers. Being efficient with our energy and time, as well as having a very specific plan of action for every hour of every day and following that to the letter is vital when we are in inhospitable terrain. Put simply, to be a successful explorer, we have to achieve efficiency in every aspect of our actions.

I learned clear lessons about efficiency on all my expeditions but none more so than when travelling to the South Pole, where there is no room for mistakes or miscalculation. For up to 60 days, my team and I were immersed in one of the harshest environments known to man, as we pushed ourselves to the limit of human endurance every day. Our home was a 6ft x 6ft tent. Katabatic winds travelling at over 100kmph blew into our faces. Temperatures never went above -15 degrees Celsius

Being efficient with energy and time is vital

and at times they reached -60 degrees. That is so cold that if you throw a cup of boiling water into the air, it will transform into snow crystals before it hits the ground.

I had to consume 9,600 calories a day just to maintain the necessary energy levels to allow me pull my sled holding the tents, fuel, food and other provisions I needed for the

We can only succeed if we are disciplined

trek. In a typical day, we were up at 6am preparing our first meal which accounted for 2,000 calories. We broke camp at 8am and then began the process of hauling our sleds for the next seven to 12 hours, breaking every 50 minutes to consume 450 calories for energy to keep moving. At the end of each day, we set up camp and ate another 2,000 calories before going to sleep to replenish our energy for the next day.

There was nothing between the coast and the Pole but isolation, ice and our objective—the South Pole, a spot in the world where all the meridians come together. Every single minute was thought out in advance and every single manoeuvre timed. We could succeed only if we were disciplined and efficient in everything we did. Success was all about getting the small details right. Our focus was locked on to our target and day after day we moved towards it.

In daily life, efficiency is also vital to get us closer to our goals. We want to complete what we need to do without wasting time, energy, resources or materials. There are, unfortunately, multiple enemies of efficiency waiting to trip us up and we often engage willingly with them.

Avoid the enemies of efficiency

Distractions are the biggest problem. Interruptions from our phones and the online world, from family, friends and even co-workers undermine our efficiency.

We need to be disciplined and take control of our environment if we want to achieve maximum efficiency. This necessitates minimising distractions and eliminating unimportant choices so we can stay focused on our priorities. To do this we need to have our day's activities set out in advance; in other words, we need to have a clear plan for our day which is enabled by a routine that works for us.

We can create routines that make the most of our time and give us maximum opportunity to be efficient and thereby reduce our stress. Numerous studies show that most of us are at our most productive in the early morning, before 11am. Before that time, we need to ensure that—where possible—we are doing the most important work of the day. This means leaving email checking, phoning, tea breaks, shopping, making appointments, along with any other non-essential tasks, until after 11am.

Productivity is less after 11am

Productivity for the majority of us lessens after the morning, so we should make sure that we are working on the most important things when we are at our most productive. It doesn't mean that the other jobs are unimportant; in fact, breaks and socialising are a very necessary component to our wellbeing on a daily basis, it just means that the other stuff doesn't need our attention when we are at our most productive.

A lot of incredibly productive people are unavailable in the morning because they are working on getting the most important jobs of the day done. They shut themselves off from the distractions of the world and stay in a 'controlled' environment to ensure maximum efficiency. They also minimise 'unimportant' choices by having a routine that they follow, no matter where they are. Many successful leaders who have very important decisions to make eliminate less important decisions that would only distract them. In the elimination process, they often start with their wardrobe and replace a daily choice with a foregone conclusion, carefully planned in advance.

Chancellor of Germany Angela Merkel's uniform is a three-button tailored trouser suit, with the main variation being the colour. She is telling the nation she has led for 11 years that she has much more important things to deal with than distracting wardrobe decisions.

Minimise unimportant choices by having a routine

Likewise, United States president, Barack Obama, only wore grey or blue suits because, he said, he had too many other decisions to make. Facebook co-founder Mark Zuckerberg has a wardrobe full of grey t-shirts and hoodies. This means he doesn't waste valuable time wondering what to wear; he has a uniform that he is comfortable wearing and spends his time and energy instead making more important decisions.

Having to make too many decisions—no matter whether they are important or trivial—leads to what is known as decision fatigue. When faced with too many choices and too many decisions, we just become exhausted and make bad judgements.

The habit of efficiency starts with:

- Minimising distractions

- Eliminating unimportant choices

- Managing your environment

- Establishing a routine that works for you and sticking with it

Once we do this, we can focus on what is really important in our day, and it's best if we do this the day before. We should know before going to bed what task we will do first thing in the morning. The beginning of the day is not the time to be deciding which task is most important. When we know what we have to do, we can focus on starting on it immediately.

Despite what we might believe, spending a long time on some task is not the most efficient use of time—the opposite is often true and whatever time we assign to a task is the length of time we will take to do it. When the same task has to be completed in a shorter time, we find that is possible. This should lead us to question our own habits regarding efficiency and productivity.

Most of us have idiosyncratic ways of wasting time on a daily basis and yet we wonder where the day, or even the week, has gone and how come we haven't done whatever it was we'd hoped to do at the start of the week. The warning bells should sound when we find that we are working around the clock and still not completing tasks or reaching our goals. At this point we are, without doubt, inefficient.

Know what needs doing and do it

To regain the habit of efficiency:

- Write down tasks in order of importance; the physical act of writing something sends a strong message to the brain that is missed if you just think about something

- Create a timetable for your day: this doesn't have to be elaborate; keep it simple and achievable but prioritise and do the most important tasks first

- Focus on keeping a calm mind and steady mood; studies show that people are less efficient when in a bad mood or feeling negative

- Have a plan: when you have a plan, you act; without a plan, you react

At the end of each day, we need to rest, switch off and refuel. Most of us don't give ourself enough switch-off time, or we don't use that time in a way that sustains us for the next day. Eating well, exercising, hanging out with family and friends, having a hobby or pastime are all good things to do when we are not working. Doing them well makes us more efficient and helps create a work-life balance that will keep us healthy and happy.

Communicate clearly to understand and to be understood

The single biggest problem in communication is the illusion that it has taken place.

George Bernard Shaw

Effective communication requires understanding that we are all different in the way in which we hear and interpret messages. Understanding and being understood, listening and being heard may sound straight-forward, but rarely are. When do we really listen to what is being said to us? When do others really hear what we are saying to them? How we communicate is something that affects our life and that of others at the deepest level. If we issue an instruction without including clear direction, we can create confusion. If we leave a message open-ended, or leave some of the detail up to the receiver's own personal interpretation, we can create confusion. If we leave blanks within the code of the message, we can create confusion.

As humans, we communicate in many ways and through many media. We speak to each other, we write to each other, we touch each other, we point, we clap, we laugh; we use various forms of technology,

Communication is a highly complex process

old and new, to communicate. We use our voice, we use our facial expression, we use our eyes, our hands, our body language; we even use silence to communicate. Human communication is a highly complex, vastly intricate process and yet the rule remains the same: to hear well, we must listen well. To be understood, we must communicate our message clearly.

In the world of exploration, we learn early the vital importance of clear communication because, on expedition, extreme conditions don't always allow for easy or immediate communication between team members. For that reason, explorers spend a lot of time before an expedition starts discussing all aspects of what might happen on the upcoming journey. Everyone needs to know what the plan is, down to the finest detail; all the team need to know what to do if something goes wrong and how communication will be maintained in challenging weather conditions. At such times, communication between team members can literally be a matter of life or death.

Proper communication with good direction is vital for success in all areas of life. We have to ensure that we prevent what is known as 'Chinese Whispers syndrome'. Chinese Whispers is a party game

Beware Chinese Whispers syndrome

where one person whispers something to the person beside them. That person whispers what they have heard to the next person. This continues until the last person is reached and says out loud what they have heard. The group generally collapses into laughter when the first person reveals the original statement which is usually completely different from the final manifestation.

What happens is that, as one person whispers to the next, miscommunication occurs for any number of reasons including inability to hear or to understand, distraction, lack of focus or general giddiness. While it is a fun game, Chinese Whispers is a useful metaphor for cumulative error and a way to highlight the unreliability of the human ability to listen, to hear and to communicate clearly.

Don't assume others understand

Throughout my time in business, I have seen good companies collapse due to the lack of a proper communication strategy. They communicate the message but do not follow through with clear directions to their teams and a proper briefing in relation to the execution of the plan. Worse still, I have had climbing friends die due to bad communication of instructions that everyone agreed to but interpreted differently. It is not enough to assume others know what you mean. There is a myriad of different conditions that could create communication blocks including fear, environment, emotion, language, culture, and habit. The greater awareness we have about the communication process, the more fluent we will become at spotting these blocks and ensuring that our message has made it through and been correctly understood.

Communication is like breathing; we do it all day, every day, consciously and unconsciously. We communicate with everyone, from those closest to us to passing strangers. The nature and quality of our communicating is impacted by many things, including our mood, our health, our age, the content of what we are communicating and our role as communicator. Although we are always in a state of communicating, this does not necessarily mean that we are effective communicators. Unless we know how to communicate successfully, there is a strong chance of miscommunication taking place. The consequences of this—in a social, family or work situation—range from annoyance

We must actively listen when others are talking

to danger. Communication is a two-way process and miscommunication carries with it risks that can impact adversely on both the speaker and the listener.

We can learn how to communicate effectively, firstly by learning how to listen well, both to what is being said and what is left unsaid. We learn a lot from body language so we need to be open to picking up messages from how people present themselves. When we listen with real attention and empathy, the speaker picks up on this and is more open and confident in their communication. Often, while others are talking, instead of actively listening, we are already formulating a response in our head. It is only by shifting our focus to better, empathetic listening that we start to really hear what others are saying.

As good listeners, we let others know that what they are saying is important and has value. Most of us know what it is like to feel that we are not being heard and the sense of isolation and exclusion that can follow. Not only do we need to be good listeners, we also need to be good speakers. As parents, employees, managers and leaders, we should consider how we communicate what we want to say to others. Communication is vital in all aspects of life, but when it comes to business, Forbes has rated communication as the most important skill in today's workplace. Before we speak, we should consider how those listening will hear what we want to communicate. This will help us focus on the manner in which we communicate our message.

- Be very clear about what you want to say and how you are going to phrase it

- Don't jump in with your opinion before the other person has finished talking

- Keep your language simple and uncomplicated

- Maintain eye contact

- Be aware of body language—your own and that of your listeners

- Avoid offensive comments or phrases

- Inject humour into your communication wherever possible and appropriate

- Check that you have been understood clearly and that those listening have the same interpretation as you

We should avoid being judgemental, both in our listening and in our speaking, in order to minimise the possibility of conflict arising and to maximise greater openness. There are few of us who haven't memories of something said in the heat of the moment that we regret afterwards. Communication is most effective when we are calm and clear so it's always best to step back from a situation where emotions are running high and take the necessary time before responding.

- A dependable way to open up good communication is to break down the barriers between people at the very start by sharing stories and laughter

- It is good to have a communication 'safety valve' system that allows you check that all has been clearly communicated

- Clear communication is a way of stemming rumour and allowing people to know as soon as possible what is actually going on; it is not good when people hear important information second-hand

- Speak to be understood

- Listen to understand

I have the power to:

- Be efficient, disciplined and decisive

- Be a clear communicator

- Listen well

- Not be egotistical

- Create a good work-life balance

- Not be judgemental

HOW TO NEGOTIATE CHALLENGE

Every journey we undertake, every goal we plan and pursue has challenges that we will need to deal with. Learning to do this effectively is a process that takes time, commitment, focus and courage. Assessing risk, being alert to danger, managing crisis and conflict, and dealing with adversity are all abilities and skills that we can acquire and master so that we become effective at negotiating challenge.

IO

Risk: cultivate your risk-taking ability

Danger: approach with the utmost caution and skill

Objective dangers: avoid where possible

Crisis: manage crisis effectively to ensure the best possible outcome

Conflict: find and maintain the balance between disagreement and conflict

Adversity: in adversity, focus on survival and getting through

Risk: cultivate your risk-taking ability

Life is a risk-filled journey and everything we do has some element of risk in it. We are always trying to minimise the degree of risk in what we do so that we feel safer, but the fact is that we can never fully eliminate it. Nor should we want to; risk is full of possibility, both good and bad. If we don't embrace risk, we exist in a kind of stasis, or inactive state, where nothing much happens. If we fear risk, we remain in the same position, unable and unwilling to move forward. Risk and challenge are part of every aspect of our life—personal, work, social, family, adventure.

> **Risk is full of possibility, both good and bad**

Our mind is conditioned to see the risk in everything we do. When there is the possibility of threat or danger, of injury or loss, of making a wrong decision, of looking stupid, or of failing, many of us take the easy option and do nothing. We ditch our dreams, goals and aspirations without ever daring to achieve them. We lose our chance to buy a new home or car, to take a holiday, to change our job, to fall in love or to climb a mountain, all because we are afraid to take a risk. We have become an increasingly risk-averse society, the result of which is a dampening of our enthusiasm for challenge. We have to change our mindset and develop a strategy that empowers us to tackle the risks that are inherent in every worthwhile goal.

Children love risk. They challenge themselves in all sorts of environments—in the classroom, the playground and on the street. They love all kinds of sports and athletics and challenge themselves to push their boundaries, even when playing games for fun. Children quickly develop risk-taking skills. They do, of course, suffer injuries, cuts and bruises and at times get hurt but they learn important life skills by being allowed to develop the ability of self-assessment in the risks that they take. As children learn about risk taking, they push their limits to

> **Develop a strategy to tackle risk**

succeed and don't back off; such skills are invaluable throughout life.

However, as we get older, we frequently lose the skill to personally assess risk due to social conditioning which tells us that we should avoid risk. Our activities in the home, school and in the workplace are increasingly curtailed. Adventure is increasingly regulated with demands being made for guarantees that there is no risk involved. The end result is that we are no longer learning how to deal with risk or to challenge ourself outside the box that we are put into. Because of regulation, most of us can no longer assess risk confidently as that

Observe, evaluate and analyse the level of risk

task has too frequently been taken out of our hands. The consequence of this is that we all live safer but smaller lives.

When, however, we learn how to calculate risk, we move forward in confidence because we have dismantled our fears. When calculating the risk of a situation or undertaking, we should

sit down and look at all the possible outcomes of taking a specific action. By engaging in this risk-calculating process we are, in fact, learning caution and creating a safety strategy for ourself. We observe, evaluate and analyse the level of risk and come up with a procedure to deal with it. We can feel exposed when we take a risk but we need to acknowledge that risk-taking is not easy and demands a level of engagement that teaches us to be courageous.

No matter what we are undertaking—whether it's making a meal or preparing to climb a high-altitude mountain—the risks need to be assessed and dealt with. Only when that is done should we proceed. If, for whatever reason, we are unable to calculate the risk involved, then we shouldn't proceed. Proceeding in such circumstances can take us into the danger zone where risk is no longer calculable and where the chances are more highly stacked against us.

When we assess risk, put our strategy in place and start moving, we put ourself in a place where achieving is possible as we journey towards our goal. Most people who make informed, calculated risks don't regret it. Even if they don't reach their goal, achievers make sure they know the risks so that they can prepare and have the best chance of success. The more we familiarise ourself with risk and how to calculate it, the more we put ourself on the line to achieve our goals, and the more likely it is that we will succeed.

- Accept that there is risk in everything you do

- Learn how to calculate risk

● You will never achieve if you don't risk; you might if you do

● There is a gamble involved in taking risks but it is always worth taking that risk once you have calculated it

Danger: approach with the utmost caution and skill

The danger sensation is exciting.

Ayrton Senna

Before setting out on expedition, adventurers spend a lot of time studying, anticipating, analysing and preparing for the possible and probable risks that lie ahead. We look at the known risks, assess them and identify the risk level acceptable to us. On expedition, this means ensuring we are mentally and physically prepared for the journey ahead; that we bring the right clothing, that we have all the food that will be needed; that we have reliable weather forecasting and communication systems.

As a leader and manager, when I take on any new project, my first job is to outline to my team the dangers associated with what we are doing. This is particularly relevant in business and adventure where risk applies and where making mistakes can be costly and, at times, fatal. We spend time planning and researching about others—both those who have succeeded and who have failed—who have gone through similar experiences in the same field. Once we have collected all the available data, I brainstorm with my teams and we decide on the rules we require as individuals, a team or organisation to minimise the risk of failure. We create a colour-coded rules indicator which becomes our template for making decisions around the risks we will encounter.

- **The Green Zone:** this is where everything is in our favour—the weather, ground conditions, health feeling good and mind is relaxed. The team is moving well from camp to camp and the likelihood of an accident or injury is low. This means that our overall objective is low risk and our goal is achievable.

- **The Amber Zone:** here we are close to or just above our calculated risk limit. We now have to be very careful to ensure that we don't go to the Red Zone where the risk is gone beyond acceptable limits. In the Amber Zone the team's antenna is raised and caution is required.

- **The Red Zone:** this is an area where danger exists and we have exceeded acceptable levels of risk. This may happen due to reasons completely outside our control or due to carelessness by team members. Once in the Red Zone, risk is no longer calculable and action must be taken to reduce the impact by putting controls in place, or by retreating back to the Green Zone.

On the world's highest mountains, a clear danger zone exists when climbers enter what is known as the Death Zone. Here, due to the nature of the relationship between air pressure and extreme altitude, climbers can only take in about 30% of the oxygen that is normally taken in at sea level. Many of those who have died on Mount Everest and other 8,000-metre peaks have lost their lives in the Death Zone. It is impossible to know in advance how you will react to conditions at this altitude, even if you bring bottled oxygen with you, as many climbers do. Everyone in the Death Zone—where your body is, essentially, dying—is affected by conditions there, and even the strongest will struggle to remain conscious and think logically. Here, danger is everywhere, even when climbing conditions are perfect.

There is an allure to danger

There is an allure and excitement for climbers in going beyond the area of calculated risk to the place where they really pit themselves against the elements. They know the stakes are high—often a matter of life or death—so, when they enter the Death Zone they make every preparation possible. Total focus is necessary, allied with the courage (or folly, as some might consider it) that comes from a determination to win against the odds. Confidence is vital before entering the Death Zone; if you don't believe that you have a chance of surviving, then you shouldn't enter it.

> 'Better a live donkey than a dead lion'

Having had to retreat from the South Pole when he was within 100km of it, Ernest Shackleton said 'Better a live donkey than a dead lion' when asked about the failure of the expedition. He recognised the Red Zone and retreated. I, too, have been happy to consider myself a 'live donkey' on occasion. I have personally known 50 climbers who have died on mountaineering expeditions or in climbing accidents and this fact alone sharpens my resolve to be alert to risk and danger.

You don't have to go to the extremities of the Earth to find danger zones; they are all around us. As individuals and as a society we do our best to protect ourself from danger. As a species we are constantly evolving psychologically and physically to detect danger. The 'fight or flight' response kicks in when we perceive danger in our environment. However, we sometimes ignore the signals and enter danger zones without taking any precautions. If luck isn't with us, the price we pay may be very high. Although the best advice is to stay away from dangerous situations, sometimes we have to go through danger to achieve our goals, and sometimes we want to put ourself in danger areas for the thrill of pitting ourself against the ultimate odds.

- Learn the difference between imagined and real dangers

- In as far as is possible, assess the risk ahead

- Recognise the difference between perceived and real dangers

- Before entering a danger zone, talk to someone who has been there already and learn as much as you can from them

- Exercise caution in danger zones

- When you find yourself in a danger zone, tap into your willpower to survive; start making decisions and act on them

- Do not become frozen by fear

Objective dangers: avoid where possible

When we start working on our goals and projects, we sit down and attempt to calculate to the best of our ability the risks involved and the possible dangers that we might encounter. We identify the areas of risk and see how we will negotiate our way through. The danger zone is somewhere most of us will try and avoid as far as possible as it's the area where we can no longer calculate risk and where the chance of injury and loss is greatest. Another area that we need to consider, though we rarely do, is that of objective danger.

Objective dangers are something that all adventurers are familiar with. They are dangers which cannot be controlled and in the presence of which one's skill levels and experience don't count for much, if anything at all. For mountaineers, the most common objective dangers appear in the form of avalanches, serac falls and landslides. The only thing adventurers can do is be aware of the possibility of objective dangers and to be vigilant.

Objective dangers are unstoppable

Objective dangers also exist in the world's populated regions and are on the increase in the form of tsunamis, floods, drought and hurricanes. We can't stop them happening; all we can do is be vigilant, hope they don't happen, and take all reasonable precautions. Likewise, in life, things sometimes happen to us individually or as a collective that we don't see coming (or we do but cannot stop) and over which we have no control. The existence of such dangers is sobering but should not stop us living the life that we want to live.

Crisis: manage crisis effectively to ensure the best possible outcome

Even before going on expedition, adventurers spend a lot of time learning about what to do when things go wrong. We accept the fact that there is always a chance that a 'perfect storm' might occur where nothing goes according to plan. It is not possible to be in the most isolated and hostile parts of the planet without having considered in advance the possibility of the worst-case scenario arising and how it will be dealt with. Preparedness is everything in these situations; without proper training and preparation, the probability of death being the outcome increases significantly. If a crisis arises, the leader and the team members know exactly what steps to take. This doesn't always ensure survival, but it does ensure the best chance of it. At the extreme ends of the Earth, we cannot run the risk of chaos taking over.

Likewise, in our personal and professional lives, we need to think about what to do when things go wrong, as they inevitably will. The nature of life in all its complexity makes it unlikely that any one of us will go through our life without encountering a crisis situation from time to time. Something will go wrong—we may not know why—and a situation will arise that threatens our stability and safety, or that of our family, our workplace or our community. A crisis is not an everyday problem and is defined by its unexpectedness, its inherent threat to destroy and/or destabilise, the uncertainty it creates and the potential it has for far-reaching consequences.

There are many reasons why crisis situations arise:

- Bad leadership/management practice

- Being insufficiently informed/trained for the task

- Ignoring internal and external warning signs

- Addiction by one or more people to the drama of a crisis situation

- Over-confidence

- Complacency

To deal effectively with a crisis, we need to have a plan and this plan should be in place long before a crisis arises. The plan should be followed closely; the middle of a crisis is not the time to be trying something new *unless* no part of the existing plan is working. As in so many other areas of life, clear and honest communication is vital in times of crisis. Those affected need to know what is going on and what is going to be done to try and regain stability. Whether it is within a family, a community or a work group, a crisis should be dealt with by everybody coming on board to support the management effort. Outside help should also be called upon if needed. People should not feel they have to isolate themselves when they are in crisis as this exacerbates the situation.

In crisis, leaders are called upon to come to the fore and lead from the front. People want an obvious leader in these times to instigate the plan and have the confidence to see it through. The leader must firstly prioritise and ensure that anything that is unnecessary is sidelined. If we are inclined to over-extend ourself regularly, we will find ourself reaching burnout very quickly in a crisis. Juggling too many balls, in life or at work, is not helpful at any time and it is very risky in times of crisis as the ball we drop might be the most important one.

> **In a crisis, do not isolate yourself from support**

Looking after ourself—physically, mentally and emotionally—and ensuring that we are 'fit for purpose' will help us deal more successfully with crisis situations. If we are calm, confident and happy, we will be better equipped to deal with tough times than if we are anxious and stressed on an ongoing basis.

- Prioritise what needs to be done and stop doing anything which is a waste of time, energy or focus

- Communicate the details to those affected; they cannot help if they are kept in the dark

- Ask for help from outside if it is necessary

- Share how you are feeling with someone you trust

- In the middle of a crisis, focus on the solution and not on the cause; that can be examined and analysed later

While most of us want to either avoid or deal effectively with crisis situations, there are many among us who live in a constant state of fire fighting. Crisis fire fighters go from mini-crisis to mini-crisis, not ever fully resolving anything and not following through on any plan. There is a certain energy in crisis situations and some personalities get hooked on that energy and the drama that comes with whatever the latest crisis throws up. As crisis fire fighters, we experience a sense of importance when called upon to deal with the various 'fires' but are not interested in coming up with solutions and proper crisis-management plans.

Such a response does not work in the medium to long term. It is a distraction, not

Some people get hooked on crisis drama

only from proper crisis management, but also from proper day-to-day progress and productivity. Constant fire fighting is exhausting for everybody and leads to frustration, resentment and the killing of enthusiasm. Fire fighting is a kind of comfort zone where we can avoid the hard work of looking for real, workable solutions. When our confidence in our ability to lead and solve problems effectively is shaky, we are all in danger of becoming serial fire fighters.

- Look at each 'crisis' to see if it is an isolated happening or an everyday occurrence that can be dealt with by proper management

- Look at your own efficiency and productivity; if they are less than they should be, it is possible you are engaging in fire fighting

- Observe how you feel when you are fire fighting. Do you like the drama of it all? Are you the focus of attention in these situations? Does that make you feel important?

Those of us who have to deal with fire fighters have a thankless task. However, we should strive to avoid engaging with or encouraging their behaviour.

- Don't engage in the drama that is unfolding; maintain objectivity

- Try and introduce rational, well-thought-out responses

- Between 'fires' suggest the creation of a crisis-management plan that everyone has an input in creating

- Point out the advantages of avoiding fire fighting in terms of progress, efficiency and the overall impact on those affected by serial fire fighting

- Accept that problems and unforeseen challenges will arise in whatever you undertake in life.

To deal well with problems, challenges and crises:

- Have a plan

- React calmly and rationally

- Maintain your enthusiasm and an open mind

- Ask for help when it is needed

Conflict: find and maintain the balance between disagreement and conflict

In the upper reaches of the world's highest mountains, or far from civilisation in the Polar regions, although the temperatures are extremely cold—mostly far below freezing—the hot-house environment in which explorers have to live for long periods of time is an ideal breeding ground for disagreement, tension and conflict. There is endless repetition in day-to-day activities; the work is often physically and mentally gruelling without any chance of respite; food is for fuel and not for comfort; in fact, there is little comfort beyond the basics. Added to that is the boredom that inevitably manifests even though we are surrounded by some of the most magnificent scenery in the world.

No matter where human beings are, disagreement will arise. The difference is that

Respectful disagreement can be positive

this cannot go unchecked or unmanaged when we are in isolated areas. The unity of the team in these scenarios is vital for its very survival. Conflict has to be managed and resolved because, otherwise, the prospect of injury or death becomes very real.

In daily life—at home, in our social life and at work—we are constantly communicating with others, listening and sharing thoughts and opinions. Sometimes we are in agreement and sometimes not; either way, the communication continues. Our opinions are informed by our experience, interests, background and beliefs and theirs are, likewise, informed by their own life experience. Not only is disagreement not a bad thing, informed arguments coming from different places ensure that everyone learns something new and further knowledge is shared about the subject. Respectful disagreement can be very positive and informative.

Conflict must be managed

We all want our opinions to be heard, to feel that our contribution is worth something, to know that we are shaping our world in some way. If we are denied this opportunity (or deny it to ourself) for whatever reason—maybe because what we have to say is in direct conflict with the accepted beliefs of the group, with the philosophy of our place of work, or with what our more

With total opposition, conflict is inevitable

outspoken partner believes—then tension develops and starts to grow.

When tension grows, unchecked and unacknowledged, the seeds of conflict are sown. When we are in total opposition to something, conflict is inevitable. Like anger, conflicted feelings are something that should not be driven underground or sublimated; rather, conflict is something that must be managed. When well managed and dealt with in a timely manner, there can be a positive and progressive outcome.

While our default position is to *want* life to run smoothly, the fact is that it doesn't. We need to accept this and be prepared to deal with day-to-day disagreements and conflict in a healthy and responsible manner. This is easier said than done. Like anything worthwhile in life, arriving at a positive, progressive outcome demands commitment to both the process and the solution.

It is so easy to walk away

It is so easy to walk away, slam the door or sabotage something that is worth saving. In individualistic cultures, we are taught that we 'win' when we shout loudest. But this is not the best approach if we want to move forward as a team, be that within a family, social or work setting. To deal with disagreement and conflict, we must acknowledge it, anticipate it, recognise the warning signs and have an agreed system with which to deal with it.

- Having a winner and a loser is not the best resolution for disagreement; in this scenario, nobody is a winner

- All sides should aim to arrive at a mutually acceptable solution

- Open, honest communication where people feel safe saying what they believe to be true is necessary

- Respectful and empathetic listening is mandatory for all sides

- Recognise that, if you were in the other person's shoes, you would agree fully with them; therefore, strive to really understand where they are coming from

- Keep your focus on the shared goal and not on the personalities; you don't have to like someone—or even be in full agreement with them—to see the merit of their contribution towards the achievement of a shared goal

When we engage with conflict in this way, the likelihood of achieving a good outcome is much greater than if we engage in trying to 'shout loudest'. Human environments are never perfect and tension is always on the ebb and flow. Ground rules around disagreement and conflict expression and resolution should be in place and known by everybody in the family, group or workplace.

Focus on shared goals and not on personalities

- Anger, disagreement and conflict need to be dealt with directly and not ignored; if ignored, these feelings will find expression in ways that are likely to be, at best, negative, and, at worst, destructive

- Create an environment of mutual respect, clear communication and empathetic listening

- Create an ethos of making disagreement and conflict resolution something in which everyone is an equal and valued participant

- Leave power struggles outside the door

Adversity: in adversity, focus on survival and getting through

*Rock bottom became the solid foundation
on which I rebuilt my life.*

J.K. Rowling

Few of us will go through life without encountering adversity or times when it feels as if the world has turned against us. These times are defined by their hardship, misfortune, suffering and trauma. In such extreme circumstances, it feels as if there is nothing we can do and nowhere we can go to escape the storm encircling us. When we are faced with adversity, however, we *have* to go through the storm. This is not like a challenge which we can accept or reject; this is an extreme time in our life where we, literally, have to focus on survival. We have to take action. If we don't, we are doomed to failure.

During the time of greatest adversity in my life, when all that I had worked for was failing, my initial reaction was to pretend that everything was okay. I hid my pain from my family and friends, ashamed of my failure. I felt alone and thought that the universe was conspiring against me. I sat in my office all day, feeling numb, and when I went home I was agitated and depressed. I felt there was nothing I could do and my pride prevented me from asking for help. I had never experienced failure before and did not have the coping skills to deal with it. When I attempted to take my own life, I was certain that I was the only person who had ever felt as I did.

Fortunately, I had the opportunity to learn that I was not alone and, once I realised this, it was more acceptable for me to talk about what I was going through and to look for solutions. I took responsibility for the situation I was in and listed my personal failings honestly and openly. Until then, I hadn't realised how much I was driven and affected by the material things in life. I realised that my belief system was based on a shallow and incorrect perception of what was truly important.

Once I opened my eyes and my heart to the reality of my situation, I listed all the possibilities that were open to me, and there were many. I had family and friends that still loved me and who encouraged me to fight back. I had a trade as a bricklayer I could return to that was in demand and well paid; I could rent a house; I was a dreamer and I could dream again; I was alive and I was a fighter. This two-year period was my rock bottom and coming through it taught me many lessons in the art of survival. In time, I was ready to dream again and came back with greater enthusiasm and bigger and better dreams and goals for business and adventure.

If we survive and are open, we learn that out of adversity can come life-changing moments and opportunities to see with new eyes and to live a better life. When we come through adversity, we learn to seek and find opportunity, even against all the odds; we come to know ourself better and have an appreciation of the real strength of our own character.

- Accept where you are

- Focus on expanding your ability to endure

- Try to become an observer of the situation you are in

I have the power to:

- *Take calculated risk*

- *Be a high achiever*

- *Be a good self-leader*

- *Focus on solutions*

- *Deal with and manage conflict*

- *Take responsibility*

THE IMPORTANCE
OF ATTITUDE

Our attitude towards a person, a group, a situation or an event is based on how we evaluate and react to whatever or whoever we are dealing with, and can range anywhere from extremely positive to extremely negative. While there are many elements that influence our attitude to a specific situation, maintaining a balanced attitude in day-to-day life is very helpful in ensuring that we learn the habit of positivity. Choosing an attitude of happiness, gratitude, humility and caring, allied with the practice of celebration and laughter, creates a foundation of strength and wellbeing. When we make the decision to face even the toughest situations with a positive attitude, then we give ourself the best opportunity of succeeding.

Happiness: choose to be happy

Gratitude: the practice of gratitude reminds you of the value of what you have

Humility: the practice of humility helps keep your ego in check

Caring: if you don't care, don't bother turning up

Laughter: laughing improves your quality of life and bonds you to others

Celebration: mark important moments and make a positive investment for your memory bank

Think outside the box: when you get stuck in attitudes that no longer serve you, practise thinking outside the box

II

Happiness: choose to be happy

Very little is needed to make a happy life; it is
all within yourself in your way of thinking.

Marcus Aurelius

We are as happy as we decide to be. Sometimes it is very hard to accept that this statement is true because, if it is true, why wouldn't we choose to be happy all of the time? The thing is, we forget that it is always within our power to make this decision, and then we don't *make* the decision to be happy. It is so much easier to be something other than happy. Why would we choose to be happy when something horrible happens? Why would we choose to be happy if our basic needs are not being met? If we are in pain?

The reason we might choose to be happy is that being unhappy will not change the facts of the situation, but will change how we experience it. When we see people who say they are happy despite what has happened to them, we should ask if they have made a choice. Our decision to be happy comes from inside and is not dependent on exterior forces. If we don't believe this, we should recall a time when everything in our life was just perfect and we were still unhappy.

Happiness comes from within. But why should we bother being happy if life is tough and the weather is bad and we haven't enough money? Who cares? We should. When we are happy we feel better within ourself, we are easier to be with and others react more positively to us. We have all been in the situation where we have seen a gurgling, happy baby and automatically smiled at it. In contrast, we turn away from others' unhappiness, and our own sadness can also alienate us from those around us, especially if choosing unhappiness is something we do regularly.

- Decide to be happy

- Keep making that decision

- Smile, even if you have to fake it

- Exercise stimulates the 'happy' endorphins; a few minutes a day can create the foundation for a new attitude

- Plan a trip

- Practise mindfulness

- Go outside and get into nature

Gratitude: the practice of gratitude reminds you of the value of what you have

If the only prayer you ever say in your entire life is thank you, it will be enough.

Meister Eckhart

Being grateful and thankful for what is good in our life is something we need to consciously practise as most of us regularly forget to be grateful. We seem to be more 'naturally' programmed to complain about that which we don't have rather than being grateful for that which we have. Yet, studies show that the regular and committed practice of gratitude reaps proven rewards for our emotional, physical and mental wellbeing.

Being grateful is something we should practise

Explorers are well placed to learn and remember the virtue of gratitude. On expedition, we invariably find ourself cut off from the physical and emotional comforts of everyday life. Despite the allure of being in extreme regions of the world, the joy of being there is allied with a sense of loneliness and a feeling of being very far away from the people and things to whom we are emotionally connected.

Being in such isolation allows us feel what it's like to be disconnected and distant from that which sustains us in everyday life, be it family, friends or even pets. The flip side of this is that we feel a keen sense of gratitude for what we have left behind and to which we hope to return.

The deprivation for explorers is apparent at both a physical and emotional level. On an adventure, we have to travel light and few luxuries are allowed. A three- or four-month expedition will

Expeditions demand deprivation

always, once we've left the relative comfort of Base Camp, involve eating food that is, at best, functional; basically, it is fuel to keep the body moving. For weeks on end, we eat rehydrated meals as well as lots of fat and sugar in powder form in an effort to consume the requisite calories to get through the day. This is not food we would ever choose to eat when at home. Explorers fantasise about eating our favourite food and drink as we eat an evening meal of nutritional substitutes washed down by hot water mixed with protein powder. We wear the same clothes for weeks on end and personal hygiene is reduced to a bare minimum.

The net effect of this is a feeling of sheer gratitude when we reach the village where we get our first hot meal and shower. The villagers at the foothills of the world's high mountains delight in giving sustenance to weary explorers, while the latter feel both humbled and joyful by something as simple

Giving wholeheartedly reflects our interconnectedness

as good food, a comfortable bed and human kindness. Inherent in our gratitude is sincere acknowledgement of the kindness of those who are giving. This two-way relationship of giving wholeheartedly and receiving gratefully reflects our interconnectedness as human beings. However, we soon forget and start taking things for granted again. And this is why we need to remind ourself to practise gratitude.

Within the Christian tradition, people practise self-denial during the six weeks of Lent. Then, on Easter Sunday, they have the great satisfaction of eating or doing that which was denied during the Lenten period. Muslims around the world observe one of the Five Pillars of Islam when they make their annual fast during the month of Ramadan. From dawn until sunset, they refrain from consuming food or liquid and practise self-discipline in a bid to cleanse the soul by redirecting the heart away from worldly activities. Believers and non-believers alike savour things more when denied them for a period; their enjoyment is heightened and they experience gratitude.

When we say 'thank you' we anchor ourself to something positive. Studies show that the benefits of being grateful and practising gratitude are physical, mental and emotional. People who practise gratitude have been shown to be calmer, with stronger immune systems and a greater tolerance of pain than those who don't. They are more optimistic and joyful, seeing the good in smaller things, and they also feel a more compassionate connection to others and to the world in general.

- Write down or make a mental note each day of what you are grateful for

- Say thank you more often and mean it

- Be grateful, not just for the good things, but also for what you learn from challenges

- Be thankful for the unique gift that is your life

Humility: the practice of humility helps keep your ego in check

In a world that values and aggressively sells its own versions of perfection, the value of humility is often obscured and cast aside. Indeed, many of us mistake being humble as having low self-esteem and feeling somehow less than others. This misconception comes from a belief that ego is king and that we lower ourself and our self-worth if we practise humility. Humility, properly understood, is, in fact, a trait that allows us to value both ourself and others equally; neither is greater than the other. To be humble, we must deal with our ego, not by suppressing it, but by understanding that we should treat all others as our equals.

When we are ego-led, we are full of ourself, over-confident, controlling, over-reactive and inclined towards anger and aggression. If we suppress our ego, we can become depressed and withdrawn, losing our ambition and sense of self-worth. We should seek a balanced expression of our ego. Humility helps us achieve this balance

To be humble, we must deal with our ego

because, when we are humble, we see the interconnectedness of the world; we are aware of the bigger picture and of the fact that nothing is permanent. We have a keen sense that the life we have is a gift, that our accomplishments are reached through the support of others, that what we own is transient and that, ultimately, this life journey is about how we are with others.

Humble people have a knowledge and appreciation of the fractured nature of human beings and human life; they know there is no such thing as perfection and don't waste valuable time and energy seeking it. We should seek not perfection but to do our best every time, and to improve the next time round.

As an adventurer, I have learned that only the foolhardy don't learn humility. When you spend time in the most beautiful and hostile places on planet Earth, you realise the extent of both your strength and weakness in the face of nature and its constant changes. The mountain you 'conquer' today may be the one that takes you out the next time you climb it.

Contrary to what we might believe, research shows that the most influential leaders are those whose way of being is defined by humility. They admit their fallibility, own up to their mistakes, seek to

Admit fallibility and own up to your mistakes

include others and welcome their contribution as equal to their own. An inclusive atmosphere where everyone feels valued and of equal importance is one of the most important and positive outcomes of a leadership informed by humility. The leader who practises humility is aware that they don't know it all and that they can learn from their team. They are keenly aware of their own limitations and, yet, because they see others as equals, they are not threatened by that or by encouraging others to self-lead.

Caring: if you don't care, don't bother turning up

In our increasingly individualistic and distraction-filled world, it is easy to give lip service to caring about those around us. Unless we genuinely care, and are genuinely cared for, life can be a hollow and sometimes harrowing experience. When we operate from a place of genuine care, it increases our connectedness to others. The opposite is also true and we experience isolation when we feel that people don't *really* care.

Really caring for a person, a group or an idea, demands commitment. Just turning up and ticking boxes is not enough. We often hear people asking about the 'quality of care' that people are receiving, especially those who are ill. We should concern ourself with the quality of care we give and receive in all areas of our life. Genuine care and nurturing are things we need every day, not just in times of illness or crisis.

- Have real empathy for others

- Have the back of those you care for

- Be attentive to people's needs

- Have compassion for what others are going through

Laughter: laughing improves your quality of life and bonds you to others

It is said that a day without laughter is a day wasted, and there are few—if any—who would disagree with this sentiment. When we laugh, all sorts of positive things happen. Even if we are faking it, our brain doesn't know the difference and the action of laughing sends a message to it that releases endorphins that make us feel better. We are more relaxed and the physical act of laughing forces us to see the funny side of something we are taking seriously, maybe even too seriously.

A day without laughter is a day wasted

It's very easy in our busy world to not have fun or take breaks from work, from exercise, or from our diaries. What we should be doing is building fun and break times into our everyday life. Life can be very tough and thankless if we don't laugh regularly; even if we love what we are doing, we still need to laugh about something and, better still, to share that laughter.

We should always beware of the danger of taking ourself and our life too seriously. It's important to focus on building up a memory bank of laughter and fun times that will cause us to smile again, long after the moment has passed. Most of us have some of those moments in our memory banks already. Our face automatically breaks into a smile when we think of them and our mood becomes more light-hearted.

Don't take yourself too seriously

The content in this 'bank' is priceless and we should make it a priority to increase those 'savings' for the future. When we smile and laugh more (and if we are out of practice then spending time with children is a good way to re-learn the habit of having fun) the benefits are all positive.

- When people smile they appear more attractive and more approachable

- Smiling demands that you relax, even if only for a moment

- Laughing releases happy endorphins which are good for you

- Laughter relieves pain

If we find we have 'wasted days' in our life, days when we haven't laughed, then we need to consciously focus on finding something that makes us smile and laugh more often. It doesn't matter what it is: re-runs of old comedy shows, spending time with people who make

Find things that make you smile and laugh

us smile, reading material that brings light into our life, playing games that we enjoy.

No matter where we are or what we are doing, we need to ensure that we take regular breaks during the day and try and ensure these are times of levity where possible. The value of tea and coffee breaks is multifaceted; they offer the opportunity for time out, for bonding with friends and colleagues and for laughter. They also give our brain a chance to rest and refuel before we return to our work.

Taking longer periods of time out for enjoyment and general down time is really good for us. It allows the opportunity to process what we have been working on and space for us to subconsciously gain perspective. It also allows time for rest and refuelling. It is very important in life to have time to 'do nothing' because, while we are doing nothing, our brain is getting a chance to process all that we are dealing with when we are doing stuff.

Celebration: mark important moments and make a positive investment for your memory bank

As children we were always up for a celebration; it didn't matter whose party it was, what time it was on or who was going to be there—as long as there were games to play and sweets to eat we were in. It's hard to pinpoint exactly at what time in life this *unquestioning* acceptance of celebrating fades and disappears, but there is no doubt that, by the time we are fully grown, we are no longer quite so ready to join in general celebrating.

There may be valid reasons for not wanting to turn up to each and every shindig or party, but when we become too choosy we start missing out on what is, in fact, an important ritual that sends vital messages to our brain about our life and the lives of our loved ones, friends, team or colleagues.

When we take the time out to celebrate something—big or small, a one-off event, or a birthday—we are telling ourself that this moment is important enough to be recognised and applauded. This, in turn, allows us register the effort and progress needed to get to this point. If a winning football team didn't register its success and celebrate it in some way, the momentum of winning is lessened, if not entirely lost. Likewise,

> # Take time out to celebrate significant moments in life

with birthdays, if we don't in some way mark our years on this Earth, then we lose sense of the ongoing journey that is our life. How can we really know how much time is passing if we don't take time out to mark significant moments?

Marking the moment creates memories that form the basis for our life stories and allow us to remember more easily. Celebrations serve as memory triggers and because they take place at a time of, hopefully, joy then the remembering process can start from that positive place.

On expedition, adventurers always take small items with them for days that are marked out in advance for celebration. On the long walk to the South Pole, which can last up to 60 days, adventurers will celebrate any birthday that occurs during those days and any national holiday from their homeland. They will also celebrate reaching certain points on the white expanse en route to the Pole. Without these markers along the endless snow and ice, it would psychologically— and therefore physically—be much more difficult to stay motivated and continue making progress.

The explorer Ernest Shackleton considered celebration a vital component on his expeditions. During the almost two years that he and his crew were stranded in the Antarctic region, Shackleton ensured that they continued to celebrate, even when it seemed there was nothing to celebrate. No

> # Move away from daily concerns

matter how little food they had left, or how unappetising the food was, an effort was always made for a crew member's birthday. They also marked national holidays and festivals. Why? Because it raised the spirits of the men who needed to believe that they would survive.

By taking time to celebrate, to have fun and to laugh, people are compelled to lighten up, to move away from daily concerns and worries and to relax. Celebrations create a space which allows us get a bit of distance from what we have been doing and, by distracting us, we have a chance to gain perspective before re-engaging with our tasks and concerns. Celebrating is also very important for recognising what we—as individuals, as a family or a team—have achieved, and those celebrating with us share in that recognition. This reinforces a sense of accomplishment which spurs us on to even greater endeavours. If we refuse to celebrate, then nothing ever seems worthwhile and motivation is lost.

Colleagues and teams celebrating together—be it to mark a birthday or the completion of a big project—allows people to get to know each other and develop greater bonds, as well as acknowledging the contribution of not just the team but each individual on it.

- Never underestimate the positive effects of celebrating annual milestones and once-in-a-lifetime achievements

- Celebrate what you can in whatever way you can

- Share your celebration where possible

Think outside the box: when you get stuck in attitudes that no longer serve you, practise thinking outside the box

To make good progress it is vital to have a plan, to be disciplined and focused, and to get rid of distractions in our life. However, we need to remain open-minded to the new and unexpected, and especially to ways of seeing the world that don't come naturally to us, leaving space for such influences to shape how we proceed. This involves learning to approach situations differently and to think outside the box that we normally think within.

We instinctively know what our 'box' is; it's that place where we have tools and ways of analysing things that we find effective and that suit our way of seeing the world. Within our box we know there are certain things we would never do. We don't always ask ourself why, we just accept the way that we usually do things. But our way doesn't always work,

Approach situations differently

or may not even be the best way. It is most likely that it is not the only way and so, by thinking outside our box, we learn new ways—maybe better ways—of solving problems, of dealing with issues, of moving forward and making progress.

With effort, we can learn to see and think about things differently. It's not necessarily easy and it certainly takes us outside our comfort zone, but unless we consciously train our brain to come up with more than our usual solutions and opinions, we will not progress and expand our horizons. If we keep putting the same ingredients in, in the same quantities, we will end up with the same meal.

To become creative in our responses, we need to get out of our comfort zone and put ourself in a place where we feel uncomfortable. Then we can tap into our curiosity and start asking questions about why we are feeling like this and see if our answers shine a light on a new way of thinking.

Train your brain to come up with new solutions and opinions

- Do something you have never done before

- Learn a new and difficult-for-you skill

- Be spontaneous

- Assume that you are wrong and go with that assumption

- Assume that another approach is better

- Really listen to other people

- Go to the cinema, the theatre, art galleries and other spaces where the creativity and imagination of others inspire you

- Read good books

- Challenge your body and give your mind a rest

I have the power to:

- *Be happy*

- *Choose my attitude*

- *Celebrate my achievements, big and small*

- *Have real compassion*

- *Laugh readily*

- *Be spontaneous*

FIND AND MAINTAIN BALANCE

A balanced approach to life is the best approach. Sometimes we need to spend a bit more time at work and at other times we need more time off, but, overall, striking a balance between both will ensure that we make good progress on our goals while also having time for family, friends and a social life. Likewise, when it comes to our emotional life, maintaining a healthy balance between emotion and logic helps keep us focused and able to make well-thought-out decisions.

Money is an important part of our life and one which we can often hold extreme attitudes towards. We should choose a responsible attitude towards money, both how we earn it and how we spend it. As we move closer towards the perfect balance between our skills, challenges and rewards, we move into an energy or flow where we can experience periods of being the person we are capable of being.

12

Don't sacrifice your life at the altar of work

Find the balance between emotion and logic

Make money serve you

Be smart about how you achieve growth

There is always a price to be paid for false economies

Be responsible

Develop good social responsibility

Time spent in the zone is a time of perfect flow

Don't sacrifice your life at the altar of work

'Work-life balance' is a much bandied-about phrase. That is because so many of us spend so much of our time striving for that balance. We promise ourself and our families that it is our newest resolution and yet we fail, for much of our life, to achieve and maintain a good work-life balance. Studies from the US, one of the most work-driven countries in the world, show that over 90% of professionals work more than 50 hours a week, with half of them working over 65 hours weekly. This results in increased stress for workers which impacts not only on work life, but also on home and social life. Mental health groups are concerned that people who do not have a good work-life balance are at risk because of the pressures that arise when we have an unbalanced life.

> We are working longer hours than ever before

We are working longer hours than ever before because the technology that makes our life easier has also created a world where it is possible to never really 'leave' the workplace. We can always plug in, check up on what's happening and do just another bit more. The result is that we never really switch off. Blurring the boundaries between work and the rest of our life is a dangerous thing; it is a slippery slope and, once we start sliding, it can be very hard to get back to a place of balance again. It's as if work is addictive.

There are many reasons for this addiction to excessive working, including fear of losing our job, fear of having our commitment to work questioned, or of being overlooked for promotion. We may fear our colleagues getting ahead of us in a world where new developments seem to happen in an instant, and if that 'instant' is when we have switched off, then we lose out, or so we believe. However, when we don't have a good work-life balance, our mental health can suffer, along with our relationship with the people in our life.

> There are many reasons for this addiction

When you work too long, the following outcomes are likely:

- You find it difficult to be happy at work, even if you like what you are doing, because it is taking up too much of your life

- You can become stressed and depressed because you feel you can't control the situation

- The more time you spend working, the harder it is to switch off when you leave the workplace

- You neglect other areas of your life, such as overall health, fitness, friendships and family time

We all know how we feel when we are overworked and we know that it's not a good place to be. To achieve a good work-life balance we need to be alert to the actions we can take immediately to redress the balance.

- Make a decision about what time you are going to stop working and stick with it

- Prioritise your jobs for the day and be rigorous with yourself when it comes to not wasting time on unimportant tasks

- Take proper breaks; get some fresh air during your break and leave your workplace for half an hour if possible

- Try not to bring work home but, if you have to, be very specific about the amount of time you spend on it; try and do it when your family are not around; don't work in the room where you normally relax

- Remember that all work and no play makes us dull; inject energy into your body and mind by exercising, having hobbies and hanging out with friends and family

Employers have a role to play in ensuring a work-life balance for their employees. Progressive companies want their workers to 'work smart' and not 'work long'.

This can be done in environments where:

- There are clear and agreed policies about not overworking

- The links between overworking and stress are acknowledged

- There is a policy of open communication so employees can say when they feel overwhelmed

- The company is constantly monitoring the working environment to ensure that employees are not put under undue stress

- Employers believe that happy workers are more productive

Find the balance between emotion and logic

When we start planning something new, the fuel that fires our imagination is our emotions. We start dreaming of what we want, or a goal we would like to achieve. We might feel excited and happy, then anxious and fearful as we imagine what it would be like to have our dream come true. We need our emotional fuel to fire us up and keep us moving.

Emotions are defined as a mental reaction, accompanied by changes in our body and in our behaviour and usually directed towards a specific object. In any one day, we can go through a wide range of emotions and it sometimes feels as if we are on a roller-coaster controlled by our emotional responses. We need to learn how to engage with our emotions in a way that serves us well, by seeing the value of emotions finding suitable expression and by not allowing our emotions to colour our ability to make rational decisions.

In any one day, we can go through a wide range of emotions

Adventurers learn that the emotional energy that fires up dreams of going on expedition has to give way to reasoned thinking when we are actually on the expedition itself. How we feel has to be secondary to getting through the challenges of the day and keeping our goal in sharp focus. In daily life, too, the key is to find a balance between emotion and reason (the power of comprehending, inferring or thinking in an orderly, rational way). Our emotions ignite our passion and our want, while our reasoning allows us follow through in a focused, efficient manner.

To achieve a healthy and balanced emotional life:

- Acknowledge emotions when they arise

- Name them

- Be curious about why a particular emotion has arisen at a given time; try and observe the sequence of events or thoughts that give rise to the emotion

- Detach from the emotion

Detaching can be the really hard part. We seem programmed to not only stay attached to our emotions, but to feed, nurture and keep them alive, even long after the event has passed that prompted the emotion in the first place. Whether they are positive or negative, we need to detach because emotions are impermanent and we have to move on from them.

Practising detachment doesn't mean ignoring our emotions, it means being mindful of how we experience them. We feel the emotion but we don't *become* it. We can feel anger but we don't have to become consumed by our anger; we can just recognise and accept it as a valid response.

Reasoned, rational thought sometimes feels like the dull sibling of our emotions. It demands that facts are looked at and assessed. Our rational

Don't let emotions consume you

side is always looking for the way forward; it has no interest in staying stuck in an emotional field. Our aim, of course, is to strive for a good balance between emotion and reason. In this place of balance, we allow the expression of our emotions while remaining detached and using our reason to inform our next action.

We want to be in control of how we express ourself and how we act, no matter what is happening. If we get too caught up in the emotional side of something, or if we shut down our emotional response and focus only on the rational elements, then we limit our ability to be strategic and curtail our potential for learning.

In 1995, I was on Mount Everest's north side with James, a young climbing partner. We had just reached the Second Step, the most feared barrier on the north east ridge of the mountain. There was a hanging ladder in place, fixed there by previous climbers. When we got to the top of the ladder, we had to unclip our ropes and swing across a sheer face in order to move up the mountain. It is a place where one cannot afford to make a mistake or it will mean death. It was at this point, also, that we could see the body of a climber who had died earlier.

I was climbing in front and had made the move from the ladder to the higher ground. When James got to the top of the ladder, he froze and couldn't make

Fear threatened to overwhelm him

the next move. Every time he took his hand off the ladder, he'd grab it again; he became unsteady and lost his confidence as the emotion of fear threatened to overwhelm him. I tried to talk him onto the higher ledge, encouraging him to make the move. He could see the summit from where he was, but he was in sheer terror. I was upset at leaving him but we had discussed this earlier and agreed that one would go ahead if the other couldn't. I knew he was strong enough to turn back and descend the mountain.

Fear was subdued by his logical mind | After a brief discussion, I continued upwards. I reached Mike, our other team member, and took one final look back. I was surprised and delighted to see James walking behind us. I had no sooner turned my back than he'd made the move. For several minutes, however, his fear had overcome his rational mind. He was well able to make the move once the emotion of fear had been subdued by his logical mind.

All feelings and responses pass. When we accept that fact, and realise that we are more than the emotion we are feeling, then we are in a much better position to achieve balance between our emotions and our rational mind.

Make money serve you

To know that you have enough is to be rich.

Lao Tzu

Money is a very emotive subject and has been the source of much violence and pain in our world and, yet, we continue to equate its accumulation with happiness. Once we accept the fact that money will not make us happy (though it may allow us live more comfortably), we can start to look realistically at the role it plays in our life. We can examine what our attitude to money is and how we can improve our relationship with it.

Remember that:

- Everybody needs money to live

- Money should serve you, not the other way round

- If you spend your time and money wisely, you will have more of both

Human beings' desire to accumulate wealth is age-old and, over the generations and across diverse parts of the world, wealth has been—and continues to be—measured in different ways. In the West, it is measured generally by one's net worth and is displayed through the ownership of property, modes of transport, jewellery, artwork and lifestyle. Ownership of wealth confers on people the option to buy exclusivity, as defined by those selling it. This lifestyle comes with a plethora of rules and regulations about what is and is not suitable for an exclusive lifestyle.

A wealthy lifestyle also creates barriers that have to be maintained between the super-rich and others who are excluded from the exclusive lifestyle. At the other end of the scale, there is poverty and hunger for even basic human needs such as food, water, housing and education. Here, the lack of money ensures that the poorest people experience exclusion, not exclusivity.

Most of us spend time worrying about money

Most recent studies show that the gap between those with the most money and those with the least is widening all the time. A small number of people are coming into ownership of more and more of the world's wealth, while a growing number are, simultaneously, living in dire poverty.

The scales are not balanced, and balance is the single most important attribute we should apply to our attitude to wealth and money. This is difficult, not least because most of us spend some period of time—if not most of the time—being stressed and fearful that we don't have enough money.

While our worries may be well-founded, studies have revealed that there is an annual amount that we need to maximise our opportunity to live a comfortable life and that figure is approximately €70,000 or $75,000 for an average household. Some of us might need a little more and some a little less than this yearly average to fund what we actually want and need in our life. Generally, beyond this amount, the study carried out by Elizabeth Dunn and Michael Norton found that any additional money earned did not add to people's happiness or comfort. The positive effects of money no longer applied beyond this amount, the research found.

So, how come we are so caught up with money, with never having enough and wanting more even though we may not actually know how much we have or need? It is due to our emotional relationship

Decide how much money you need to live your life

with money; an unhealthy relationship that is fuelled by fear, greed, the market and those whose business it is to sell. We are better served if we turn down the dial on our emotions and fears and take a good long look at the facts and figures of our financial life. We should establish what amount of money we need to live the life we are living (or the life that we want to live). Once we know the amount of money that we need then we can work towards reaching it.

The ironic thing is many of us are already there. When we analyse what it is we really want and exclude that which we are currently wasting our money on, we can re-balance the scales and make informed decisions about what we really want to spend. Knowing exactly how much we need each year to pay for our day-to-day life and save for the future allows us to create the foundation for a realistic—and not fear- and emotion-based—attitude to money. With this information, we can decide the life we want and plan how to fund it, whether that involves earning more or less money.

Are you misspending?

We should also look at our spending habits. Are we buying things we don't want or need, thereby misspending our money? If so, a change in direction will allow us to use our money for what we *really* want and need. If we find that we are cash-rich and time-poor and that we are not managing to have time with family and friends, then we need to find the balance here, remembering not to put it off until it is too late as so many people do.

We should not be led by the offer of more money if the price we have to pay is our freedom to live a full life. It is only difficult to say no to an increased wage when we don't acknowledge what we are being asked to sacrifice for the extra money. We can never buy back the time we don't spend with those who are important to us.

- Try to earn enough to live the life you want

- Know how much you need to live the life you want

- Don't misspend your money or your time

> ● Realise that having more money than you need for the life you want won't add to your overall happiness

I often tell the following story which is a modern-day parable that encourages us to wake up to what we want, what we have, and how we want to spend our life:

An American investment banker was at the pier of a small coastal Mexican village when a small boat with just one fisherman docked. Inside the small boat were several large yellow-fin tuna. The American complimented the Mexican on the quality of his fish and asked how long it took to catch them. The Mexican replied, 'Only a little while'. The American then asked why he didn't stay out longer and catch more fish. The Mexican said he had enough to support his family's immediate needs. The American then asked, 'But what do you do with the rest of your time?'. The Mexican fisherman said: 'I sleep late, fish a little, play with my children, take siestas with my wife, stroll into the village each evening where I sip wine and play guitar with my amigos. I have a full and busy life.'

The American scoffed. 'I am a Harvard MBA and could help you. You should spend more time fishing and, with the proceeds, buy a bigger boat. With the proceeds from the bigger boat, you could buy several boats and, eventually, you would have a fleet of fishing boats. Instead of selling your catch to a middleman, you would sell directly to the processor, eventually opening your own cannery. You would control the product, processing and distribution. You would need to leave this small coastal fishing village and move to Mexico City, then LA and eventually New York City, where you will run your expanding enterprise.'

'But, how long will this all take?' the Mexican fisherman asked. 'Fifteen to 20 years,' the American replied. 'That's the best part. When the time is right you would announce an IPO and sell your company stock to the public and become very rich. You would make millions!' 'Millions? Then what?' the fisherman asked. 'Then you would retire,' the American said, 'and move to a small coastal fishing village where you would sleep late, fish a little, play

with your kids, take siestas with your wife, stroll to the village in the evenings where you could sip wine and play your guitar with your amigos.'

Be smart about how you achieve growth

Achieving and maintaining growth is something all groups want to do. Expansion is good but there are dangers in expanding at a rate that is faster than we can deal with, or expanding just for the sake of it.

Beware the dangers of rapid expansion

When we start a business, we hope and expect it to grow, but we need to manage that growth very carefully so that we are not overwhelmed and end up losing everything.

Avoid the pitfalls of over-expansion by:

- Adopting a steady pace

- Having a clear plan and revisiting it regularly

- Closely observing the bigger picture

- Not rushing into every new opportunity without analysing it carefully

- Not being ruled by greed

There is always a price to be paid for false economies

The high price that is to be paid for false economising by cutting corners is a hard lesson that adventurers learn in harsh environments. Going on expedition is always expensive and some adventurers lose their life when they economise on vital items such as clothing and footwear. They may have great tents, ropes and enough food at Base Camp but are let down by unsuitable clothing when an unpredictable weather event arises and they become stranded on the higher reaches of a mountain.

People have frozen to death because of false economising. There can be no compromise in certain areas; for the adventurer these areas include food, clothing and equipment. In our everyday life we should be very wary when it comes to making a 'saving' and remember the cliché that 'If it seems too good to be true, it probably is'.

Be responsible

The price of greatness is responsibility.
Winston Churchill

While we have our first lessons in responsibility at a very young age, learning to be truly responsible is a lifelong lesson. In our early years, we gradually learn to tidy up after us, to take care of our pets, to be careful with our toys, to be responsible for ourself and our stuff. As adults, we learn that being responsible is a choice: we can either choose to respond in a responsible or irresponsible way to what each and every day presents us with. It is often much easier

Being responsible is a choice

to choose to not be responsible; being responsible demands a stepping forward and declaring ourself to be accountable for what is happening. Sometimes, it just seems easier to let someone else do that, whether we are operating as an individual or as a member of a group.

The downside of not taking responsibility is that we are not seen as people who can be depended upon or trusted to carry out important tasks. We lose the opportunity to become people whom others admire and want on their teams and in their lives. When, on the other hand, we choose responsibility in all areas of our life, we become known as people who can be depended on, who are reliable and who don't seek to hide in the crowd or leave the burden of responsibility to others. This affirmation from our peers helps us grow in confidence and self-esteem.

- Do the right thing, morally and legally
- Do what you have said you will do
- Take responsibility for your actions
- Own up to your mistakes
- Don't seek to blame others

While choosing to behave responsibly can result in hard work (and the more responsible we are, the more responsibility we will usually be given), the positives far outweigh the negatives.

- Responsible people and corporations are taken seriously by others
- Responsible people are admired and trusted
- Responsible people are rewarded in many ways

When we decide to consistently behave responsibly, we empower ourself by stating that we are active agents in our own life. We don't engage in a blame game because that is, ultimately, a waste of time. As responsible people we are more interested in solutions than in blaming others when things go wrong.

\# Develop good social responsibility

Some of the earliest lessons we learn in life are about looking out for others, being responsible and being accountable. We often forget these lessons as we grow older, and even more so when we seek to create distance between our actions and their consequences. In recent times, we are—as adults—learning again the lessons of minding and looking out for people other than ourselves. This is especially apparent at corporate level, with more and more companies committing to corporate social responsibility (CSR). CSR is a form of self-regulation built into a company's best practice framework. CSR not only adds to a company's public image as studies show that it can also help increase long-term profits.

Corporate social responsibility can help profits

Some believe that committing to CSR for greater profits can be a cynical ploy where companies do good solely to offset any negative environmental or social impact they might be creating, as opposed to having a commitment to eliminating negative impacts. It is hard, however, to argue against the positives to be had from any commitment towards a heightened sense of social responsibility. Committing to CSR brings greater acknowledgment of a company's bottom line, broadening it out to the 'triple bottom line' (TBL) of its social, environmental and financial impact.

More and more companies, especially in the high-tech arena, build in the TBL to their company's business model from the start. They are proud to say that, as a business, they want a better world and they want to make a positive impact. Apart from being global business leaders and internationally successful companies, the likes of Microsoft, Google, The Walt Disney Company, BMW and Apple are also recognised as leaders in the development and implementation of CSR.

Enacting corporate social responsibility can be as simple as running an annual fundraiser for a local charity in the community to donating a percentage of

Many companies want to make a positive impact

yearly profits to education projects locally or elsewhere. Committing to sustainability, even if it is not cost-beneficial immediately, is another example of CSR. Aside from it being a conscious commitment to doing and creating good, there are other benefits.

- CSR builds links with the community where a company is based

- CSR helps to create a positive public image locally, nationally and internationally

- Employees feel part of something bigger and more important than commercial enterprise alone, which can increase their commitment to, and respect for, their employers

- There are possible long-term financial benefits

We have never had more information available than we do now about the interconnectivity of everything in the world. What each one of us does has an impact. When it comes to large groups and companies, this impact is huge. With such power comes the need for responsible behaviour towards people, towards the environment and towards how money is made and spent. The lessons our parents and grandparents taught us about looking out for each other, putting our rubbish in the bin and helping those less well off are lessons we can apply at every stage of our life.

With power comes the need to be responsible

We know the power of one; how much greater is the power of many, especially when we embrace genuine corporate social responsibility? After we are gone, after our corporations are gone—no matter how successful or long-lasting—their social, cultural and environmental impact will continue to resonate and reverberate. It is up to us to ensure that impact is for the benefit of those who journey with us and who will follow when we are gone.

\# Time spent in the zone is a time of perfect flow

After months and years of training and learning, a climber may find themselves scaling some of the most challenging and dangerous terrain in the world and be totally at ease while doing so. It might seem strange that, at the point when the challenge is at its most extreme, the climber is at their most engaged and confident. This is a time of 'flow', of being in the zone, where there is a well-struck balance between challenge and the skills needed to meet that challenge.

We can all attain a state of flow

The terms 'flow' and being 'in the zone' are ones we usually associate with athletes, artists and creative people. The singer appears to embody the emotion of the song they are singing, the dancer becomes the dance and the footballer seems to move beyond normal human constraints to take on another form and become fluid in the movement of the game. This, according to the psychologist, Mihály Csíkszentmihályi, who brought the current understanding of 'flow' to the world, is a state of happiness, of feeling alive and a full expression of our strengths.

When we are in the zone, or in a state of flow, we are enacting the most authentic expression of our true self. This state is not something that is only available to renowned artists or successful athletes. Achieving a state of flow is something we can all attain. It is a state we should aspire to because it is in 'flow' that we will find most happiness. In flow we are closest not only to our true self but also to our best self.

When we are in flow, we are at our most creative and productive. We are

In flow, we are at our most creative

fully engaged with what we are doing and doing it to the best of our ability. We cannot be engaged in some activity beyond our skills and simultaneously be in a state of flow, because flow is only achievable when there is a balance between the challenge and the skills brought to that challenge.

After many decades of researching flow, Csíkszentmihályi found that, at its simplest, flow can be described as 'total immersion in what one is doing while having very clear goals, immediate feedback and a balance between challenges and skills'. When all these elements are present and we are engaged with the challenge, then we are at the point of being most in tune with who we really are. It doesn't matter what the activity is: teaching, cooking, climbing, performing surgery, cycling, running, painting—the list is endless. What matters is that the elements Csíkszentmihályi lists as being necessary for flow are present.

Flow happens when there is balance between challenge and skill

We might be good and skilled at lots of different things, but there might be only a handful of things that we do where we feel we are getting into the zone of flow. A key ingredient for achieving flow is passion. Those of us who have passion for what we are doing are much more likely to move into the zone of flow and experience happiness and joy. When we are in a state of flow, what we are doing is important to us because it is the only thing we want to do and achieving the various clear goals of the task is important.

When we are in flow, we will stay at a task no matter how long it takes or how difficult it is to the point of not even noticing how tired or hungry we have become. The clarity of our goal and the passion we have to stay with it sustains us, because it is all that matters at the time.

When we bring the components necessary for flow into our daily life we can become more effective and happier. One of the greatest obstacles to achieving this, however, are the distractions that fill our days and compete for our attention. We are connected to so much at any one time that it is difficult to focus on one thing only at a given time. There are so many choices to be made and so many options available that our energy gets depleted.

Passion is a key ingredient for achieving flow

If we can limit the number of activities that we undertake in any one day, and do this over a sustained period, we can focus more effectively on the smaller number of tasks that we want to undertake. We can start to give them our complete attention, to engage fully and with passion and so create an environment where flow becomes possible.

Employers are increasingly finding that when employees are exposed to flow conditions in the workplace they are happier and more productive. Being given clear tasks or goals that reflect the correct balance between skills and challenge, with immediate feedback and sufficient freedom from distractions to complete the task allows employees to thrive, even at tasks that are not overly interesting.

The more we are in a state of flow, the more we are in a place where we are achieving optimally, the more productive we are and the happier we are. In flow, we get better and better at whatever it is we are doing, learning more and expanding our knowledge all the time. Csikszentmihályi warns, however, that the flow experience is good only insofar as it allows us experience life in a more meaningful and intense way, permitting us to learn and improve our skills. As with all things in life, flow must be managed and used as a tool to enhance life: the zone is not a place where we remain full-time.

I have the power to:

- *Work smart, not long*

- *Have a good balance between logic and emotion*

- *Not sacrifice my life for money*

- *Live responsibly*

- *Develop a social conscience*

- *Experience flow*

THE INEVITABILITIES OF LIFE: HOW TO DEAL WITH THEM

Life's inevitabilities are like the ebb and flow of the tide. We make new habits for a new life and then they become old habits that may no longer serve us. We finally get what we have worked so hard for only to become complacent and forget that nothing ever stands still; we win, we lose, we achieve victory, we suffer defeat: such is the tapestry of life. In order to be the best explorers that we can be, we need to learn how to deal with the inevitabilities that an ever-changing life and world present.

I3

Keep good habits, get rid of bad ones, make new ones

Complacency fogs your vision of how to do things better

Obsession is, ultimately, your enemy

Failure is the benchmark of a worthwhile apprenticeship

Define what success is for you and work to make your life successful

Assess the situation and have the courage to change course when necessary

Rise up after each defeat and try again

You win when you challeng yourself to be the best that you can be at any given tir

Keep good habits, get rid of bad ones, make new ones

Our life is shaped and coloured by our habits—the things we do, day in, day out, repeating them to the point that we are no longer even aware of them. Our habitual actions are part and parcel of how we arrange our time to complete what it is we have to do within a particular period. We form habits by repeating the same actions time and time again to achieve the same result. For example, to get to work punctually we engage in a series of habitual actions that help us achieve the goal of arriving at our workplace at a specific time every day. If something unexpected happens, if we sleep in or traffic is heavier than normal, we can feel that the order of our day has been upset.

Good habits can become bad habits

For practical reasons, there is an absolute value in having good routines in our life. However, we can become slaves to routine, so much so that we might not realise that our daily routine is no longer serving us. If we don't examine our habits and how they are serving us and shaping our life, then good habits can become bad habits, and bad habits can limit us and our potential for achieving.

All habits are born out of repetition. Yet, most of us find existing habits hard to break and new habits hard to make. Anyone who has ever tried to lose weight, to learn a new language, to be nicer to people, to get up earlier and go for walk before work knows this well. If, for example, we really want to get healthier and fitter, we probably need to change our eating habits. We make a plan for healthier eating and achieving a fitter lifestyle, then one day we feel tired and buy our favourite take-away food. We feel guilty and disappointed with ourself and might give up altogether on our new plan. A fierce internal self-talk takes place when we revert to our old habit and we might even decide that it's not worth trying to break the habit because we believe we haven't the willpower to do so.

All habits are born out of repetition

In this instance, we let a habit that is no longer serving us shape our life in a way we don't want. But we shouldn't give up; the more often we practise a new action or behaviour, the more likely it is that it will become habitual. Falling into our 'old ways' doesn't mean that the pattern of the new habit disappears from our brain, it only means that it hasn't been practised sufficiently often yet for it to become the dominant habit. We just need to keep practising and keep focused on our new goal.

It takes courage to create a new habit

A company manager I know attended weekly meetings with other managers and found that, week after week, the same topics were coming up and little was ever being resolved. She noticed that nobody was taking minutes at these over-long meetings which were taking place in a small, stuffy room. People were unco-operative at the meeting because the room was too warm and airless and nobody remembered what they were meant to do because nobody had been assigned the task of taking minutes and sending them to those in attendance.

Resentment grew among those present. The manager decided that change was needed. All agreed with her plan to have shorter weekly meetings in a cool hall where everyone would stand and present their information in bullet-point format. Minutes were taken and forwarded to everyone within a few hours of the meeting. Old, unproductive habits were broken and replaced by new, effective ones.

It often takes courage to create a new habit, especially within a group where engaging in habitual behaviour—even if the behaviour isn't helpful—creates a sense of belonging. However, we shouldn't be afraid to risk introducing our group to new ideas. These could include bringing healthier food into the workplace or going for a run during the lunch break instead of hanging around and falling into a common trap of negativity and complaining. Once we see the benefits that others are getting from new habits, it's likely we, too, will follow as our interest is triggered.

It is the same with our thinking, which can be as habitual and routine as our actions. If we keep having the same mental reaction to situations and people, we can never move on from these scenarios and never see different potential in them. We need to be courageous in examining our mental habits and ask if they are serving us or limiting our ability to see the opportunity in a situation or the positive traits in a person. It is good to attempt to see things from a different perspective. If we approach a situation or a person with a new mindset, we find that something new will happen. This action is especially good if we feel that we are stuck in a rut. When we respond differently, the 'rut' will change.

- Examine habitual behaviour

- Examine habitual thinking

- Keep good habits for as long as they serve you

- Don't be afraid to get rid of old habits that no longer serve you

- Adopt new habits just for the fun of it and see where they lead

When we are open to change and welcome it into our life we begin to see new opportunity all around us. It is out of random moments that the most radical change can come and we should be open to reacting positively to that change.

Complacency fogs your vision of how to do things better

The tragedy of life is often not in our failure, but rather in our complacency; not in our doing too much, but rather in our doing too little; not in our living above our ability, but rather in our living below our capacities.

Benjamin E. Mays

The first part of the Cambridge Dictionary definition of complacency sounds good. It is defined as 'a feeling of calm satisfaction with your own abilities or situation'; the second part of the definition, however, is not quite as reassuring—'that prevents you from trying harder'. Complacency is hard to recognise unless we are alert to it. It is a place that feels comfortable and pleasant; we find we'd like to stay there.

We have come through the ups and downs of our journey to get to this place of 'calm satisfaction', a place where we can breathe a

Complacency is the enemy of progress

sigh of relief in the knowledge that we are finally in the driving seat; we know what we are doing, we have the necessary skills and all is under control. In the land of complacency we are doing exactly what we need to do, and probably doing it well.

What's the problem then? The issue with complacency is that it is the arch enemy of progress. When we become complacent, we stop moving forward; we accept everything as it is, for better or worse. Complacency reflects a loss of engagement, passion and energy. When we become complacent, we are like people walking around in a bubble who can't see what is going on around them.

In high-altitude climbing, no matter how good the conditions are or how skilled we are, if we become complacent we put ourself in danger because objective dangers—such as earthquakes or avalanche— that cannot accurately be predicted, are everywhere. Likewise, in everyday life and business, there are objective dangers to startle and surprise us, and if we relax into complacency we are either going to be hit by them or overtaken by people who are more actively engaged in their journey. We need always to remain alert to the change which is constantly happening.

It is a fallacy to believe that what is working for us today will work forever; it won't. There are many stories of well-established

We must remain alert to change

companies who never move with the times and are oblivious to both the dangers and the opportunities around them. When we look at the Kodak and Nokia stories, we see two giants of their industries who were complacent and failed to innovate. These one-time leaders in their fields didn't see the change that was happening around them until it was too late. Nokia was too slow to react to the growing market influences of Android and Apple technologies, while there are few corporate failures as written about as Kodak's failure to see the change that was coming with the growth of digital photography. The result was the destruction of its film-based business.

When we are complacent, we cease to be really energised. We may be doing well, making money and having a good lifestyle, but we are no longer exploring the limits of what is possible. If we fall into the complacency trap, then we lose our edge and focus, we stop looking at the bigger picture and eventually get by-passed by those who are more alert and hungrier than we are.

- Always be on the lookout for new opportunities and possible dangers

- Embrace risk

- Innovate or die

- Just because it 'ain't broke' doesn't mean it isn't past its sell-by date

Obsession is, ultimately, your enemy

Many adventurers have sustained terrible injury or lost their lives to summit fever. 'Summit fever' is a term used in high-altitude mountaineering to describe the mindset of a climber who finally has the summit within his or her sights and who is gripped by a determination and obsession with reaching it, no matter what. Those in the grip of summit fever engage in actions that are highly dangerous and potentially life-threatening. Debate continues to rage about climbers on the highest mountains in the world who, despite extreme frostbite and not having sufficient oxygen, continue upwards and never make it down again because of summit fever. There are further stories of those who have walked past injured climbers and continued on their way to the summit, leaving the other person to die.

Despite all the warnings, even the most experienced and sensible adventurers can be infected by summit fever. The journey to the top of the highest mountains on Earth or to the furthest extremes of the Poles is not easy or cheap. When we are within reaching distance of our goal, it is tempting to disregard all warning signs, especially when we tell ourself that it's just another hour, another few steps, that we're almost there, that we can do it, that we don't mind losing a finger or a toe or that, after all the effort, we don't mind losing our life.

Eleven climbers died on K2's deadliest days

In early August 2008, 11 climbers died during what is now grimly known as 'K2's deadliest days'. K2 is the world's second highest mountain and is considered to be the 'mountaineer's mountain' because of its extreme technical challenges, its unpredictable weather and an infamous and hazardous overhanging wall of ice, or serac, under which climbers spend time as they move up through a treacherous ice gulley known as the Bottleneck. On 1 August, after many days of bad storms, there was a break in the weather; it was a 'perfect day' and men and women who had been on the mountain for months took their chance to get to the summit.

The bad weather and now this perfect weather window meant that, before long, there was an unmoving queue in the Bottleneck, a place where nobody wanted to spend time. Above the sweating climbers, the lethal serac was glistening in the sun as it melted, making it increasingly unstable. Sometime around 10.30am, a Serbian climber fell to his death from the Bottleneck. A few hours later, there was a second fatality, most likely as a result of altitude sickness.

The sensible thing would have been to descend

The remaining climbers were in a dilemma. The sensible thing would have been to descend but the wait had been so long, the cost so great and now, here they were, on a perfect day and the summit was within a few hours' reach. *The Summit: How Triumph Turned To Tragedy on K2's Deadliest Days*, a book I wrote with Pemba Gyalje Sherpa, describes how summit fever took hold of many of the climbers. It tells of the dilemma in which Pemba, a member of the K2 Norit team who would go on to become the 2008 National Geographic Hero of the Year, found himself as he struggled to get climbers to descend following the first death on the mountain.

Pemba ... began to feel deeply uneasy about what was happening around him ... Climbers had carelessly unclipped from fixed ropes, some had mindlessly overtaken their peers, and others were panting heavily and floundering on the ice, evidently ill-prepared and inadequately trained for the physical demands of the terrain ... Pemba was exercised about the physical limitations of many of the climbers and concerned about their ability to reach the summit. The further into the Death Zone they climbed the more compromised they would become ... Enough had gone wrong, he thought, to make him believe that the summit attempt was not meant to be; it was time to consider a retreat.

Pemba stalled, drifting to the back of the line of climbers and allowing them to ascend ahead of him, partly to reflect and gather his thoughts, and partly because of the dangers along the fixed lines. His dilemma was now acute. He felt deeply apprehensive about progressing, but he also felt that he owed his team a loyalty and commitment to assist in any way he could to make their summit bid a success. The pressure on him to advance further was palpable, entrapping him in the desire of others to proceed.

Over the next 36 hours another nine climbers died, either on their way to the summit or while attempting to descend in the dark.

None of us would normally say that we would be happy to injure our body or lose our life to achieve a goal. None of us would think that we might walk past someone who needed help, saying that the next person will help them, or that we will help them on the way down, or that their predicament is their own fault anyhow. Yet, in the grip of summit fever, this is the mindset that takes over. It is a place where rules and ethics are cast aside to achieve our goal.

> It is a place where normal rules are cast aside

In daily life, we can liken summit fever to a dangerous obsession that blinds us to all else and which has the potential to destroy our life. It is where we start to neglect and ignore our own code of conduct or rules for living in order to pursue our goal. Summit fever makes us both vulnerable and neglectful of ourself and others and should be avoided at all costs.

Failure is the benchmark of a worthwhile apprenticeship

Failure is not the opposite of success; it's part of success.

Arianna Huffington

Failure is an 'F' word that we don't like to use in our everyday talk. We don't like to talk about failure but we *need* to talk about it and stop treating it as a source of disgrace or embarrassment. Failure is not the opposite of success, it is part of the journey towards achievement and success. Giving up is the opposite of success.

- Everyone will fail at something during their life

- Failure is an intrinsic part of taking on new challenges

- You learn more from failure than you do from easy success, both about the process and about yourself

- You neither let yourself nor others down when you fail

Failure is an intrinsic part of the journey to achievement. We encourage children to keep learning when they start to walk and talk and read. We never think of them as failures as they embark on their earliest journey of learning. Why then, as adults, are we so hard on ourselves and on others when we fail? When we are learning, we are trying

Failure is part of achievement

to find out what works and what doesn't work. Sometimes we find out quickly and sometimes it takes a lot longer, depending on circumstances.

Failure is hard, but it is not shameful. It offers opportunities for learning and when we see it as a natural part of our journey through life, then we become open to the valuable lessons it has to offer. If we have never failed, it is likely that we have never really tested ourself or pushed ourself to the limits of our capabilities. When we fail, then we know that we are trying, that we are attempting to realise our goals, to achieve something, to make a difference, to succeed.

Learning how to approach failure and to examine it for the knowledge and insight it offers is something we need to do if we are to progress beyond the feelings of shame and despondency that are traditionally associated with failure. We need to programme our mindset to see the positives of failure, such as the opportunities to learn, to come up with a better approach and to develop an even better strategy.

- Failing is an opportunity for learning what works and what doesn't work

- Have a positive mindset regarding failure

- Be compassionate towards yourself and others who fail

When we know that we are going to fail, that we will not reach our goal this time round, we should disengage from the emotions of disappointment and despondency and focus on what we can learn and enjoy in the process. There are very specific reasons why we fail, some to do with ourself and others that we have no control over. If we can manage our emotions during the time of failing and afterwards, then we will gain valuable insight into our own limitations and the nature of the challenge we have undertaken.

Following failure, we need to acknowledge our feelings but not indulge them; they should be kept in perspective and we must keep an eye on the bigger picture. Once we step back from our emotions, then we can start to objectively assess what caused the failure.

- Were you ready to undertake the task?

- Were you properly trained?

- Did you have all the necessary skills?

- Did you want to succeed in the undertaking?

- How great was your want to succeed?

Then we continue; we do not give up unless the risk it too great. We reassess, we engage with what went wrong, we re-group with our network, our team and our mentor. We find support where we need it.

There are very specific reasons why we fail

We maintain our passion and when we learn what went wrong, we make another—better—plan.

When my business failed, I had to accept that, in order to survive, I needed to learn the lessons it had to offer; otherwise I would have made the same mistakes again and again. After losing all of my wealth, I went back to being a bricklayer, something I wouldn't have thought possible when I was a successful property developer. I started, literally, from the ground up again, rebuilding my life and business block by block.

I learned that you can always start over; that the most important thing with failure is to accept it and not to be defined by it. Failure isn't the end; it is the beginning of a new chapter if you learn the lessons it offers and seize whatever opportunities are available. My

My failure forced me to think outside the box

failure forced me to think outside the box, to see things from another perspective. Instead of feeling hostile towards the bankers, I learned to negotiate with them and found that when I approached them with a different mindset, they were open to helping me. Most importantly, I sat down and analysed the mistakes I'd made and resolved never to make the same ones again.

Define what success is for you and work to make your life successful

Success is no accident. It is hard work, perseverance, learning, studying, sacrifice and, most of all, love of what you are doing or learning to do.

Pelé

We all want to be successful; it's as simple as that. No matter what we do, from the most simple, straightforward thing to the most complex undertaking, we want to succeed. Booker T. Washington, the author and advisor to American presidents, said that, 'Success is to be measured not so much by the position that one has reached in life as by the obstacles which he has overcome'.

To want to succeed is instinctive, to attain success is another thing entirely, and while everyone wants to succeed, not everyone wants to do what is necessary to attain success. Succeeding is hard work; being successful continues to be hard work; remaining successful is even harder work. It doesn't ever get easy. So why do we want it when all it seems to be about is hard work?

Success can bring with it many things that people cherish—feelings of accomplishment, fame, adulation, wealth, influence, access to **We all want to succeed** other successful people, admiration, a feeling of importance. When we decide that we want to be successful at something, no matter what it is, we can't sit back and wait for it to happen. We must feel our want, ignite our passion, make a plan, set our goal and start working.

Even with its allure, many people decide that success is way too much hard work and that they'd rather not work so hard. We can't give the level of commitment that total success demands to everything we do. In fact, it's a good idea to take up something we have no vested interest in succeeding in just so we can have some time out from the hard work needed in the area where succeeding is our prime motivator.

Our successes, from the small to the large, from the insignificant to the significant, give us a taste for more. Each success builds our self-confidence and self-belief. Each success acts as a block on which we can build as we learn more about the process of succeeding. Especially when we are not succeeding in one area and are feeling down-hearted, it is vital to do something where we can achieve

Many decide that succeeding is too much hard work

a measure of success as this will rekindle our self-confidence and self-belief. If we find that we have run into what feels like an immovable wall and we are really stuck, some time out doing something entirely different, such as learning a new skill or taking up a new hobby, allows us space to reignite our self-confidence.

Maintaining focus and motivation is vital in achieving success and so, too, is being 100% committed to getting over the line, despite the effort, the long hours that have to be put in, the inevitable boredom that arises or the desire to throw in the towel. There were times when I was training for my Everest attempt and would climb Carrauntuohil—Ireland's highest mountain—three times a day in order to stay fit. For Polar trips, I spent up to two hours every day over a three-year period pulling tyres through dirt tracks in our local forests in the effort to become quicker, faster and more efficient.

Whenever exhaustion, boredom or the sheer effort threatened to overwhelm me, I would imagine what it would feel like when I achieved my goal and this visualisation kept me motivated. Giving up was not an option and the thought of what success would feel like helped me endure the slog.

Success is best when shared

The route we take to success should be one that we are completely happy with; if we have to compromise ourself in a way that undermines our ethics or moral sense, our success will be tainted. When we achieve success, we should be mindful of the dangers that can come with it. We must ensure that we view our success realistically and incorporate it into our life in a way that enhances it and the lives of those around us. Sometimes, success can destroy our life or we may not realise until too late that the price we have paid has been too high. Keeping an eye on the bigger picture will help us keep a good perspective. Success is sweetest when the road is shared, enjoyed and celebrated.

Assess the situation and have the courage to change course when necessary

We make plans based on the information we know and on what we expect to arise in the future. Good plans are grounded in fact and knowledge and, the more knowledgeable we are, the better we can prepare for the journey ahead. No matter how well-prepared we are, however, we must constantly assess our plan because, in life, there is constant flux, with new and unexpected situations arising. In high-altitude climbing, for example, plans are constantly assessed and reassessed because of objective dangers and unpredictable weather conditions. Climbers have to always expect the unexpected. They must be prepared to react immediately to whatever is coming their way because lack of preparedness can mean death.

Climbers have to always expect the unexpected

When conditions are not as we had planned for, then we need to be able to react quickly and decide the best course of action. We may need to wait it out or, if conditions change totally, we may need to amend our route and our plan. When we assess ourself and our plan regularly, we check in with how we are feeling, mentally and physically, about our progress and about what lies ahead. We find out if we are strong enough for the next part of the journey, or if we need to take some time out. If our strength is not what we need it to be, we must act on that knowledge, knowing that the unexpected could happen and put us in a place of danger.

There is always more than one route to our destination and sometimes, following reassessment, we see that we need to change from the route we are on, for one reason or another. There is the usual and most obvious route and that is the one we will most likely set out on but that may not always be the one that best suits us. When we realise this, we should not fear or regret having to take another route to our destination.

There are many routes

The biggest danger is that we will abandon our goal when the route we have been on, or the route we thought we could travel on, is not the one we can take. So, when we are making our plan and looking at the road to our goal, we should also keep an eye out for alternative routes, just so we know where they are if we need to take them.

As well as being open to changing our route when it is necessary, we must also be open to retreating if that is the most advisable option.

Battles have been won after strategic retreat

Most of us don't like the idea of retreating without having reached our destination, but sometimes it is the wisest and safest thing to do. If we find, after a reasoned assessment, that continuing is dangerous, then it is time to consider a retreat back to base or to some place where we can rest, replenish our energies and regroup.

Many a battle has been won following a strategic retreat. Retreat isn't defeat. Ignoring warning signs, however, is foolish and potentially dangerous. If, for whatever reason, the outlook is no longer good and conditions have become totally unpredictable, then the wisest and most courageous thing to do is to retreat.

In 1996, Goran Kropp, a young Swedish man, had cycled 13,000 kilometres and climbed to within 100 metres of the summit of Everest when he made the decision to descend due to low energy levels and the impending dark. He knew he had reached his limit and that his energy levels weren't sufficient to get him safely to the summit and back down again. He knew the mountain would always be there and that he might lose his life if he didn't retreat when continuing was dangerous. Three weeks later he tackled the mountain again, this time summiting successfully.

Persisting on our journey when the signs are telling us to stop and return to base or to take time out can exact a very high price on our health, our life and our business.

- Constantly assess progress and how you feel on your journey

- Have the courage to retreat when the signs tell you that continuing is not the right thing to do

Rise up after each defeat and try again

While one may encounter many defeats,
one must not be defeated.

Maya Angelou

It is inevitable that, in life, there are times when we must accept defeat. Nobody likes it and how we handle it determines how we progress on our journey. Many great lessons about how to handle defeat come from observing sports teams and athletes. We would be shocked if our favourite team decided to disband following a defeat; we expect and demand that our sports heroes dust themselves off and try again. It is that which makes them heroes in our eyes; they try and they persevere.

> There are times when we must accept defeat

Sporting defeats are shared by sports-people and their followers. Everyone who is invested in the game experiences the emotion of the defeat. The players and followers take time to express their feelings, they analyse what happened, what went wrong, how it could have been done differently. Everybody affected processes the experience and then they start preparing for the next competition. They are not defeated by defeat. We can take lessons from the sporting arena and apply them for those times when we encounter defeat in our own life.

- There will always be another opportunity

- Use defeat as a chance to learn; analyse what went wrong, where improvements can be made, how your 'fitness' for the project was, and seek to find a new and better approach

- Acknowledge that you did your best while also accepting that your best is different on different days; next time out your best might be much better

- Do not be defeated by defeat

You win when you challenge yourself to be the best that you can be at any given time

We live in a world where winning is all-important, and why wouldn't it be? Our need as humans to have our efforts validated and acknowledged by others is fundamental. From their earliest years, children present their parents with poems they have written, pictures they have drawn, and crafts that they have made. They are bursting with pride at their accomplishment and waiting to bask in the glow of recognition. Parents and teachers are most often generous in their praise and the awarding of stars and medals. They know that their children are doing their best and winning in the journey of learning.

Our need for validation from others is fundamental

As we go through life, this need for validation and acknowledgement doesn't lessen. As adults, we also want to be appreciated and to have our efforts valued. When this happens, we are motivated to continue because we feel happier and more satisfied; in effect, we feel as if we are winning at something. With a winning mentality, one where we feel we are doing our best and pushing ourself to make our best even better, we stay focused on our goals and on learning and improving.

We are curious about how we can do something better so that it becomes easier. With each successive effort, we find greater ease and skill in whatever it is we are doing. In this way, we take the holistic view that winning is doing our best, and making that personal best better with each effort as we work on improving our ability and skill.

However, especially in the Western world, the winner is defined as the person who comes first and beats all the others. This understanding of 'winning' is something that we are all familiar with and have absorbed: 'I am the winner when I come before everyone else.' The rhetoric used to promote this understanding is very compelling because it simplifies and reassures. It states that there are only winners and losers and if we don't want to be losers, then we must be winners and, in order to win, others must be beaten.

This understanding of winning creates a very competitive world where stress and dissatisfaction can be high because the definition of what is the 'best' becomes more and more difficult to achieve and sustain. In the competitive world of sport, many elite athletes resort to taking drugs to enhance their performance, because to win they have to consistently defeat all others no matter what. This is winning at any cost. Such winners are lionised, excessively financially rewarded and made into heroes. The public loves them as long as they continue 'winning'.

While society tells us that the winner is the person who takes gold, the team that wins the championship or the company that has the highest turnover,

Those who overcome most are the real winners

many of us often consider those who have overcome most to get to where they are and achieve what they have achieved as the real winners. Yet, the dominant public message about winning continues to revolve around beating others, as opposed to winning because we are succeeding against a variety of ever-changing odds.

There is a story I've heard and which I like to share about a Special Olympics team in the 1960s. Eight girls from different teams trained hard over three years to take part in the Games. Each wanted to win gold more than anything else. At the start of their race, the gun sounded and the runners sprang from the starting blocks. Almost immediately, one girl fell. Another runner stopped and turned to give assistance to her fallen competitor. The other six runners then stopped and turned. All eight linked hands and came across the winning line together and each received a gold medal.

For me, this story shines a light on something that we have lost in society: the belief that real winning is about everyone getting over the final line together. What it taught me is that winning is about being the best that you can be while helping others to be their best too. When I was in the Antarctic and we were just about to reach the South Pole, I thought of the Special Olympics

Teamwork got us over the line

story. Our four-person team formed a line and touched the Pole marker together in recognition of the fact that our strength came from the teamwork which had gotten us to the winning line.

Studies have shown that while we like to compete and pit ourself against the odds, excessive competitiveness does not make us happy.

Nor does winning in such circumstances make us happy. When we see winning as something that can be achieved through self-challenge and co-operation with others, a winning mindset becomes more

Winning is about being the best you can be

meaningful and healthy than when we see winning as something that involves defeating others or being defeated by others. It doesn't really make sense when everyone trains to the best of their ability and gives their all that they are considered losers because, on a particular day, under a certain set of circumstances, another person or team beats them. What value, then, do we put on the effort, experience and journey of the 'losers' when society tells us that only the 'winners' have value and should be rewarded? The winners, of course, will feel great and, next year, if they don't win, they will feel the opposite, even though they may have done the same training and more of it, to try and win again.

Winning and our relationship with it is complex. Wanting to win and be the best we can be is good and having a mindset that reflects this helps us to focus, to learn and to grow. We are winning when we persist in moving towards our goal, in spite of the obstacles and challenges that we encounter along the way, and in a manner that reflects our code of ethics and respects the rules of engagement. Once we tap into our want to win and take action, we set out on a journey to being winners. Each milestone reached along the way shows us that we are winning. Reaching the final destination is the point where all our efforts are distilled into a final moment of acknowledgement that we have won.

However, believing that we only win when we beat others is a narrow interpretation of what winning is. Excessive competition

We have to win ethically

forces us to see our competitors as 'enemies' and creates negativity because, if we are not better than them, then they must be better than us. We learn little about ourself when we win by competing with others; we learn much more about ourself and about life when we win by challenging ourself to be the best that we can be, taking into account the circumstances in which we find ourself.

How we win is very important and we have to win ethically. If we achieve something in a way that is underhand, illegal or not in keeping with our code of ethics, then the win is tainted. Winning at any cost is not good and such an approach ultimately damages us, our business, and our public and private standing.

- You win when you do the best that you can do at any given time

- Wanting to do your best motivates you to stay on a learning journey

I have the power to:

- *Make new habits when I need them*

- *Get rid of old habits*

- *Not be complacent*

- *Be innovative*

- *Learn from failure*

- *Ignite my passion for what I want*

THE GREATEST EXPEDITION OF ALL: LEARNING HOW TO WORK WELL WITH OTHERS

There is little in life that we can accomplish on our own; we are in the company of other people as we enter this world and, if we are lucky, as we make our final exit. In between, we meet people every day for one reason or another. They are our family, friends, neighbours, community, colleagues, carers, strangers, enemies. Learning to work with all these people is a lesson that continues as long as we are alive.

The relationships we form are both formal and informal, clearly or vaguely defined, momentary, short term or lifelong. Whether we are part of a team or learning to self-lead, whether we are leaders, mavericks, mentors or working in collaboration with others, learning how we work best together makes life not only easier but so much richer and rewarding.

14

Team player: when you are part of a team that works well the day is full of possibility

Foundation blocks of effective teams

Self-leading: self-leaders make great team members

Maverick: allow your maverick sense guide you in the search for new and better routes

Leadership: when you lead well you inspire others to make their best effort

Partnerships and collaborations help you to achieve beyond what you can accomplish alone

Mentoring: a good mentor is worth their weight in formal learning

Team player: when you are part of a team that works well the day is full of possibility

The way a team plays as a whole determines its success. You may have the greatest bunch of individual stars in the world, but if they don't play together, the club won't be worth a dime.

Babe Ruth

We form teams all the time, either consciously when we join an existing group, sports team or work team, or more gradually and organically when we start to share those attributes that make a team with other people. A team is any number of people who join together and work towards the realisation of a common task or goal. Depending on the project, the team can be made up of a small or larger number.

Synergy is at the heart of a team

At the heart of any team is synergy which is defined as a 'state in which two or more things work together in a particularly fruitful way that produces an effect greater than the sum of their individual effects'. The synergy of an effective team is like fuel powering the team to its destination. When all the elements exist to effectively synergise a team, that team will be very productive. There are a number of characteristics that define teamwork and make us team players.

- A shared goal

- Commitment from each member to the achievement of the goal

- Clear communication and agreement on how the team will progress

- Trust and loyalty between team members to the shared goal and to each other

- Organisation of the team so that each member has a specific task or tasks to carry out which constitute their contribution

- Willingness to contribute beyond assigned and agreed tasks if and when the need arises

- The expectation that each team member will show up and perform

- Mutual respect for the importance of each team member's contribution

A team needs consensus between members. For this to happen, the goal has to be clear, shared and achievable. On any team, formal or informal, communication has to be crystal clear and commitment to the shared goal has to be total. If this is not the case, the notion that a team even exists is brought into question because, by its very definition, a team is a number of people sharing a goal. Without sharing a clear vision of the goal, then the 'team' is just a number of people talking about something and thinking about doing it. When we are part of a team, we have moved beyond the talking-about-it stage to the point where we say, 'Yes, I want to do this and be part of this team'. Once we make the commitment and become part of the team, we move to the next phase.

In this phase you:

- Learn the full facts of the shared goal

- Know your role and what contribution your presence is making towards achieving the goal

- Feel that your contribution is as important as that of every other member of the team

- Recognise the importance of everyone else's contribution

- Take responsibility for showing up and performing on the team

- Share the pain and the joy, the failures and the successes of the team as a collective

Teams have positions filled by people and every position is important. Sometimes people don't realise the importance of their position, or they overestimate the importance of their position in relation to those occupied by others. Those who underestimate the importance of the role that they play may do so because they are at a lower rate of pay, or because they are, in fact, in the wrong position within the group and have skills that would be better utilised and more productive elsewhere.

> **We need to realise that every position on a team is important**

Those who overestimate their importance may do so because they are the highest paid people in the organisation or because they believe their skills and knowledge are better and more crucial to the success of the company or project. Neither attitude is helpful and such attitudes need to be challenged to ensure optimal performance and best results.

Getting people to understand and appreciate the importance of the roles played by others is important, and a radical way to achieve this is to allow them 'walk in the other person's shoes' and work alongside them for a period. Sports teams often do this in training. They challenge any possible feelings of superiority by getting players who excel in their own position to switch to a position where they are not so skilled. This has the double effect of shaking them out of any complacency that might have set in and of introducing a greater understanding of the roles played by other team members.

It is only when we see things from a different perspective and with new eyes that we truly understand that every cog

> **Every cog in the machine is vital**

in the machine is vital to keep the machine running optimally. It is difficult to appreciate the importance of the work others do unless we actually experience it first-hand, or unless that 'cog' suddenly disappears or stops moving.

A story which illustrates this perfectly dates from 1962 when the then president of the United States, John F. Kennedy, visited the NASA space centre. On a tour of the centre he came across a man cleaning the floors and stopped to speak with him. He introduced himself and then asked the man what he was doing. 'I'm helping put a man on

Ensure positions are filled by the right people

the moon,' was the man's answer. And he was. Many might think that he was just cleaning the building but he was, in fact, one of many vital team members in the project to explore the galaxy and put the first human being on the moon.

It is so important to ensure that positions are filled by the right people. If they are not, people struggle and become ineffectual at best and, at worst, repeated chaos and fire fighting ensue. When my father retired, he had some men that he wanted me to take on in my building company because they had been loyal workers for him. I agreed to take on a number of them. One older man, Timmy, had worked for my father for over 20 years. I knew him as a labourer and when I took him on I positioned him in an area which required hard manual work. I could see immediately that he was not up to the job. I wanted to fire him and told my father. He asked why and I replied that Timmy wasn't good enough or quick enough.

My father then explained that Timmy was no longer used to hard labour and that I should move him to another area. At the time I was

We all make a contribution

having problems in maintenance. Timmy had a lot of experience in this area, my father said, but I hadn't known this. I moved him to a new position in maintenance and for the next five years while Timmy worked for me, I never had another complaint.

I learned then that everybody has a position; it's just a matter of finding the right one for them. As team members, all of us make a contribution, no matter how big or small, and that contribution is part of the overall effort.

- Every position is important
- Each role carried out by a person is necessary to the successful functioning of the team, the group or the company

- Get out of your position and into someone else's if you want to really understand and appreciate their contribution

- Everybody should take their position seriously, recognise its importance and fulfil their role to the best of their ability

- Everybody's position should be respected equally by everybody else

To achieve goals, a mixture of skills and abilities is needed. No one person will have all of these and a good team will contain a balance of the skills and abilities required to achieve a goal. If there is imbalance on a team, if someone is not pulling their weight or is in some way injured or ill, that will affect the whole process and cause frustration and dissent if not addressed.

Keep the team bonded

While strengths and weaknesses of individual team members should be accommodated and extra support given if needed, when a team member finds they are not up to the task, they need to leave the team. When this happens, their contribution in helping to bring the team to this point should be acknowledged. The most important thing, however, is to keep the cohesion of the team and to continue to move towards the goal in a manner that will bring the team over the line.

The bond uniting team members is strengthened with:

- Clear and honest communication

- Shared pride in the objective

- Shared ethos of how the goal will be achieved

- Agreement on the plan

- Agreed allocation of tasks

- Outlining and analysis of risks, recognising that the team can't control all factors as it moves towards the goal

- A sense of humour which is vital for keeping things in perspective

Foundation blocks of effective teams

The foundation blocks of effective teams are a shared goal, clear communication, proper preparation and recognition of the individual contribution of each team member, with the shared goal being the cornerstone on which to build the team. Great leaders will convey to the team the emotion of what reaching the goal will *feel* like. When we visualise and tap into how we will feel when the goal is achieved, we become more motivated to achieve that goal.

Shared goals create a bond between team members

Sports teams aiming for the ultimate prize in their particular sport will have seen lots of images of other teams holding up the trophy, celebrating and sharing their win; this allows them imagine what it will be like for them to win. Likewise, we all need to imagine what success for our team will be like. How will we feel and look? What kind of expression will we wear? How will our team share its success?

While a shared goal creates a bond between team members, it is not enough on its own to really unite the team. On teams, people bond in much the same way as in day-to-day life, by engaging in simple activities together outside of worktime. Sharing mealtimes and breaktimes have long been shown to be one of the simplest and most effective bonding methods. The Polar explorer, Ernest Shackleton, made shared mealtimes a priority for the men on his expeditions. It was during these times that the team members had the opportunity to share their stories, ideas and concerns and to engage in humour which is such an effective de-stressor. In the

Humour is an effective de-stressor

workplace, breaktime is often the only regular period that people have to chat and get to know each other better.

Especially in today's world of online communication, the opportunities to talk face to face with our team are becoming fewer and fewer. When we interact directly with each other, we connect in a way that doesn't happen online, starting with the simple fact that we have to look at each other with no screen to 'hide' behind. Additionally, multiple studies have found that tea and coffee breaks not only give us a chance to move away from the demands of work but also create a space for exchanges between people which have been found to have a positive effect on productivity.

Face-to-face talk is good in our increasingly online world

Proper preparation for teams is vital and involves good training and skills acquisition. When a team trains together, it makes it possible to assess the strengths and weaknesses of the team. It also allows us as individuals to identify our own strengths and weaknesses. It is incumbent on the team as a unit, and on us as individual members, to ensure that we have the necessary skills and training so that neither team members nor the achievement of the goal are endangered.

While there must be unity of purpose and vision on a team, we must also allow for difference and individuality in team members. There is room on each team for a diverse range of people who express their passion in different ways. On teams, we should allow personalities shine through and make space for good inter-personal relations to develop. We shouldn't assume because someone is, for example, introverted, that they don't have the same passion for the goal as an extroverted person. Good team members can be lost if we don't recognise that they have the necessary want and skills, even if they don't conform to the stereotype.

Allow for individuality on a team

When a team reaches its goal, it is a time of great emotion. It is very important when the goal has been achieved to celebrate as a team and to honour the input of each member. There is often a sadness or anti-climax after the high of reaching our goal and we need to recognise this as a normal part of the process and allow space for the sense of loss that comes when a team has fulfilled its aim and dissolves.

Self-leading: self-leaders make great team members

In life we can be followers, leaders or self-leaders. We can also move between each category, depending on what task or project we are undertaking. We are followers when our interest and passion are not yet matched by our skills and sufficient training. As followers, we acknowledge that we need to be led; we don't know the terrain well

We can be followers, leaders and self-leaders

enough and are not confident of being able to deal with all the challenges that present themselves on the route. We are followers in the apprenticeship stage of our journey. We become leaders when we master our craft and learn how to use all the tools of the trade. As leaders, we match our passion with training and experience. This enables us to be confident in our own ability to lead others.

Between following and leading is the self-leading phase. As we progress in our training and learn the skills we need, we advance in knowledge and ability. However, to become self-leaders we must make the decision to adopt self-leading behaviour; many of us don't and remain forever in the 'follower' phase. This is not a problem if we are content to remain at a certain point in our journey, or prefer to advance at a more gradual pace. If, on the other hand, we are hungry to learn more and want to advance at a faster pace, then we move from follower into self-leading mode. When we do this, we make a conscious decision to observe and manage our own progress; we

Self-leading demands honesty

start taking responsibility for our actions, our behaviour, our skills level and our commitment.

Self-leading demands a high level of honesty with ourself. If we are not totally honest about our aspirations and our limits, then it becomes harder to fully self-lead. When we are self-leading effectively, we remain open to learning new and better approaches as we increase our knowledge and skill set. Integral to self-leading is the willingness and desire to engage very consciously with the process and this is reflected in our desire to contribute our own ideas and suggestions as self-leaders. As we go from being followers to being self-leaders, we learn to move from an emotional to a more rational response to the challenges that face us. It is only when we learn to be effective self-leaders that we can move on to leading others.

- Self-leaders are excellent followers because they are actively engaged in the process of learning and gaining knowledge and skills

- Self-leaders support the leader in a meaningful, constructive way which makes for more effective and productive teamwork

- When you self-lead you grow in confidence

Maverick: allow your maverick sense guide you in the search for new and better routes

There are those of us who always play by the rules and are happy to do so; we like knowing what the structure is, what our role is and what the negotiating space is. We are on the path taken by the majority and learn how to deal with both the positives and negatives of that. Then there are those among us who are mavericks, people who take nothing for granted, who challenge the rules and regulations because they want to do things differently. As a maverick, I question everything, even if it works. This is because, a lot of the time, I think things can be done better by taking a different approach.

Mavericks may have the same goals as everyone else; it's just that they are taking a less-travelled or previously unexplored route. This can cause friction with the upholders of the established order who mightn't like having the rules and order they created—in good faith more often than not—being challenged by those whom they may perceive as outsiders. Traditionalists may feel challenged and threatened by new approaches. Breaking down old systems can be painful for everyone and both mavericks and the established order are well served by taking cognisance of what the other is trying to achieve.

It can be lonely being a maverick

It can be a lonely road being a maverick. When we are outsiders or mavericks, we don't have the supports that insiders have, but we don't have the restrictions either. We can use the freedom of this space to experiment and think outside the box. There may be huge pressure to conform when we pose a challenge to the status quo. However, when we believe that we have made a breakthrough to a new and better way of doing something, or that the existing rules have become exclusive rather than inclusive, this is the time when we must remain courageous and maintain self-belief.

Remain courageous

We need to acknowledge any vulnerabilities we may have, address them and then forge ahead, having ensured that we have the skills and knowledge needed for what we have set out to achieve. We should be ready to discard old beliefs when they no longer serve us and are, in fact, impeding our progress.

I adopted a maverick approach in the 1980s when I was trying to trade out of financial ruin. I had just done a deal with my bank which had given me a licence to sell sites for houses. But the country was still in the grip of recession and my potential clients had no chance of raising the deposit needed to secure the necessary loan from their building society or bank to buy a house. So I set up a loan scheme within my building and auctioneering group and loaned the deposits to the clients myself. I then gave them a letter stating they had secured the 10% deposit for their house.

The letter ensured the building society or bank would loan them the balance of the money to allow them purchase their house. The client would then repay me the money that I had loaned them. Without this deposit, these people had no chance of getting their own homes, and with the recession they hadn't a hope of securing a loan from a traditional institution. I took the maverick route and solved a problem for both them and me.

Leadership: when you lead well you inspire others to make their best effort

Leaders become great, not because of their power but because of their ability to empower others.

John C. Maxwell

Since earliest times, human beings have sought to be led. We seek out a person with specific qualities who stands at the head of the group and shows the way. Without this leader and the leadership they bring, the group becomes unfocused and struggles to find the way forward and to make progress. We need leaders to unite us, to help clarify our goal and to oversee the creation of the path that we will travel to achieve it. Leaders are those who have—or learn—the qualities necessary to lead the group effectively. We don't have to be the best at everything to be the leader. In sports, team captains are not always the best players but are chosen for their ability to inspire and motivate the team in its pursuit of a shared goal.

There have been numerous studies on the subject of effective leadership and what makes an outstanding leader, and while people will never fully agree on what exactly makes a great leader, there are key qualities that all leaders need.

An effective leader:

- Has self-belief and confidence in their own ability to lead

- Inspires confidence and hope in their team and motivates them to act

- Has the trust of the team; to create this trust the leader must be a person of integrity with a clear code of ethics

- Treats everyone on the team equally and with respect, no matter what their role is

- Understands that team members bring different skills to the project and recognises where they are best utilised

- Is a good decision maker and is not afraid to make hard decisions

- Has a positive belief in the project and in the team's ability to reach its goal

- Assesses and minimises risk, creating a safe environment in which the team can work

- Has excellent communication skills and communicates openly about everything that impacts the group and the project

- Listens to understand and speaks to be understood

- Works hard for their team and the team's goal; respect, not popularity, is the reward they most prize

While all leaders need to have or learn these attributes, leaders do not have to keep to a rigid formula. As long as the key components of effective leadership are present, then a leader can formulate their own personal style. There are many different leadership styles and approaches informed by the personality and experience of the leader. Some people prefer a more formal style of leadership, reflected in everything from how people are addressed to codes of dress and office layout, while others prefer a more informal approach. We should not be misled by informality in terms of language and dress, however, into thinking that the leader is lacking commitment or focus.

There are many different styles of leadership

The most charismatic leaders can end up being the most divisive as it becomes more difficult for them to manage their ego, while those who are more reserved can, in fact, be hugely effective because the path ahead may often be clearer for them. Different styles of leadership highlight different qualities and responses in team members; any team under a different leader will be a different team. When we find our style as a leader, we should stick with it if it works for us and our teams.

Without followers, a leader cannot lead

Without followers, a leader cannot lead and vice versa. When leaders and followers come together, their shared energy and vision can make great things happen. It is a key responsibility of the leader to put in place a framework that allows the team to work to the best of its abilities and to flourish.

Leaders need to know their team well and invest in the team and the development of each member in order to ensure that everyone is engaged with the team and its goals. This can be achieved by connecting with members at a more personal level and by making them feel appreciated and acknowledged. A leader should know the skills levels of each team member and not make assumptions about people's skills as this can have potentially disastrous consequences if a wrong call is made. It can also lead to overworked and overstressed team members who are more susceptible to becoming disillusioned and negative. An effective leader needs to keep confidence and optimism high.

This can be done by:

- Getting the best team for the project

- Ensuring balance in the team make-up so that there is an even distribution of tasks and skills

- Having a strong work ethic

- Having a clear plan

- Ensuring that progress is reported to all team members

- Owning up to mistakes and making amends

- Inspiring and igniting the want in team members; this is then converted into self-belief and belief in the team and the goal

Trust is probably the single most important attribute that a leader needs to create among the team. If the team doesn't have trust in the leader then, at the very best, the journey will be a lot tougher and less enjoyable than it would be if trust existed. Open, honest communication is the gateway to building trust. A leader needs to ensure they are kept informed of all that is happening within their team and all that impacts on the team's ability to perform.

Trust is the most important attribute

Team members should feel secure in communicating their needs and opinions without fear of dismissal or judgement. Leaders should be confident in communicating progress to the team and take the time to acknowledge and celebrate that. A leader also needs to be able to communicate problems that arise and the risks that the team face and how these are going to be dealt with.

Every leader needs key people with whom they can talk so they can get feedback on their plans and concerns before communicating them to the wider team. Being in the position of leader is often a tough and lonely place to be; leaders should anticipate this and ensure they have the people around them who help them work effectively.

Wherever there are people, disagreement will inevitably arise. Leaders can deal effectively with this by being very clear on what is and isn't acceptable within the team's code of practice. Potential conflict situations need to be recognised quickly and managed effectively so that reaching the team goal is not sabotaged by dissent. Leaders should not be undermined by team members and, likewise, should not undermine team members. Team members should feel they will be listened to and there should be a clear communication structure in place so people know how they can safely make their feelings known.

Leaders should not undermine

One of the biggest threats to the dynamic and energy of a team is micro-managing. It eats away at the trust, confidence and enthusiasm of team members. They feel the leader doesn't believe they are fit for the job while the leader becomes stressed from overwork and exhaustion. Even when a leader believes and has confidence in the team, they destroy the spirit of the team if they micro-manage. Micro-managers appear not to be listening and not to have confidence in those around them. They overwork, re-do the work of others and don't delegate efficiently. They undermine the team bond and don't communicate their concerns in a helpful manner. This leads to confusion, resentment and disillusionment among the team, and to burnout and stress in the leader.

Leaders should always be training their team to self-lead, confident that their leadership is not threatened by creating self-leaders. An effective leader will ensure that each member knows what their task is and that they have the skills to accomplish

Micro-managers overwork, don't delegate and suffer burnout

it. The leader can trust the team members because they have given them all the tools that they need to self-lead and be a part of a successful team. When team members are trained to self-lead, they are more likely to step aside when, for whatever reason, they can no longer fully contribute to the team. As self-leaders, they can assess if they need to get off the team, change their position, or take a break for a period of time.

Sometimes leaders have to make hard calls. If the goal of the team, or the team itself, is in any way compromised by a team member, the leader has to make the final call and take them off the team if they haven't gone of their own free will. Likewise, leaders should stand down a project if they know that it is doomed. While this is a tough position to be in, a good leader will, when necessary and based on their experience and intuition, make the hard call.

In Polar exploration, there are three men who stand out for me as exceptional leaders: Ernest Shackleton, Roald Amundsen and Robert Falcon Scott. All three are renowned for their leadership qualities under the most testing of conditions. Scott was known as a dictatorial leader, Amundsen was known as a brilliant logistical leader and Shackleton was known as a humanitarian leader. Commenting on the differences between these three leaders of early Antarctic exploration, geologist and explorer Sir Redmond Priestly said: 'For

A good leader will make the hard calls

scientific discovery give me Scott, for speed and efficiency give me Amundsen but when disaster strikes and all hope is gone, get down on your knees and pray for Shackleton.' My own preferred style is leadership by consensus, with the final decision being made by the leader.

Partnerships and collaborations help you to achieve beyond what you can accomplish alone

Throughout our life we form partnerships, whether they are informal, formal, personal or public. Partnerships exist because no one person can accomplish everything they need or want to do by themselves. Sometimes we seek partners because we are lacking specific skills and knowledge, and sometimes we seek partners because we reach a certain ceiling in our growth and it is only through partnership that we can diversify and bring our ideas, talents or products to a wider market. The form that partnerships take ranges from informal to formal networks, right through to legally binding arrangements between individuals or groups. No matter what form is being used, there are key elements in every effective partnership.

- Trust

- Honesty

- Clear communication

- Accountability

- Mutual respect

In high-altitude climbing, it often happens that teams form loose partnerships with each other for roping certain sections of the mountain. The logic is that there is no point in every team setting ropes on the same terrain. Such work is always difficult; ropes are expensive and, as you get closer to the Death Zone, conserving energy is vital. For these reasons, teams will come together and share the roping of the necessary parts of the mountain.

A team leader will, however, be very careful when deciding what teams to approach and form a partnership with. If ropes are badly laid, or if the rope itself is of inferior quality, then the chances of someone dying are significantly increased. Team leaders, therefore, need to feel confident that potential partners share their focus and aim, which is to climb safely and to get back to Base Camp alive.

They ask the following:

- Can I trust this team?

- Can we get on for the time we need to work together?

- What is their equipment like?

- Does their approach to and style of working match ours?

- How responsible are they?

- How skilled are they?

- What are the costs of this partnership and are they being equally shared?

When a rope-setting partnership is formed and works well, it makes climbing the toughest parts of the mountain so much easier and everyone benefits. Likewise, in personal and business life, when we form effective partnerships, each partner gains from the support of the other. A successful collaboration of like-minded individuals or groups can bring benefits which reach far beyond new contacts and can launch the right partnership into an entirely new stratosphere.

An example of how partnership can work is as follows: a group of bakers will benefit from networking with other bakers and the retailers that stock their product.

No one person can accomplish everything alone

However, if a baker and a farmer meet and combine their bread with their free-range chickens, they may go on to produce a sandwich, opening up an entirely new product line and revenue stream. If they meet and collaborate with a healthcare professional, they may provide a low-fat, organically reared chicken sandwich on gluten-free bread which is endorsed by the keep-fit industry. This may lead to collaboration with a TV producer feeding teams for an athletics-based TV game show. The end result is that this healthy sandwich reaches a whole new market that would have been totally beyond the original reach of a farmer feeding chickens and a baker baking bread.

You need to agree a strategy

Once convinced of the benefits of partnership and collaboration, we need to invest time and energy researching the best possible partnership and creating a solid foundation. When building a partnership, we need to plan, prepare, investigate and invest ourself if we are to achieve the best possible result. Once we have selected the person or people we believe we can count on, we need to agree a strategy for the relationship that follows.

Business relationships are less about friendship and more about respect and mutual benefit. When networking for business, many of us focus instinctively on what we want to get out of the situation.

We help each other to grow

But the key to building a solid and successful business collaboration is to concentrate on helping others to succeed also. Our reward from the partnership flows directly from how effectively we help the other person to move their efforts forward.

While committing to an authentic, mutual partnership, we must also keep sight of our common goal and review whether the relationship is fulfilling its initial potential. It is not enough to build trust in a business collaboration, there must also be mutual benefit for it to succeed. In a one-sided business relationship, one partner may deliver less than expected, either through lack of skill or commitment, or by trying to elicit most from a situation without any genuine desire to contribute or add value to the relationship. While the possibility of entering a one-sided relationship should not prevent us from attempting to make successful collaborations, it should ensure that we review and run maintenance checks on our partnerships.

Review and run checks on your partnerships

To give partnerships the best possible chance of working, we need to set boundaries, goals and defined areas of agreement in advance to safeguard the investment of everyone involved.

There must be perfect clarity, with clear communication lines developed from the start. There must be a commitment to an outcome, a shared belief system and a contract to ensure everyone knows and is happy with their role. We must find the right balance between being a giver and a taker.

Find the right balance between being a giver and a taker

We must also realise that a relationship requires dedicated, consistent work and attention to ensure its continuation. Our life and circumstances will always change and we need to take account of that as we move forward with our partners by building trust and genuine respect. We need to be able to count on the people that surround us and they need to know that they can count on us. Lasting and successful partnerships don't 'just happen', they take a considerable amount of work and commitment but the right ones can be an integral and vital part of our success.

Know who you can count on

For successful partnerships and collaborations you need to:

- Build trust

- Seek meaningful connections

- Identify common goals

- Use good judgement

- Develop mutual respect

- Value loyalty

Mentoring: a good mentor is worth their weight in formal learning

The delicate balance of mentoring someone is not creating them in your own image, but giving them the opportunity to create themselves.
Steven Spielberg

Mentors are a very important source of knowledge and support in the learning process. We often focus on learning through formal means, however, and forget that learning from a mentor can be one of the most productive ways of gaining knowledge. In addition to sharing their expertise, mentors also act as supports to us during times of self-doubt, failure or loss of focus—all those times that inevitably arise in the journey of life during which the support of someone who knows exactly what we are going through is invaluable.

The mentor-apprentice relationship has existed in one form or

Mentors are invaluable

another for well over 1,000 years. Many of us meet our first mentors when we go to school and a senior is assigned to guide us through the early days in a new environment. A new employee may be taken under the wing of someone from their department who is experienced and knowledgeable and who will mentor them. Businesses are now using mentoring widely as a resource for supporting employees.

We don't have to be in a formal workplace to find and benefit from mentors. The mentor-apprentice relationship is a key one in the world of exploration. Particularly before the advent of lightweight recording equipment in high-altitude climbing and Polar adventure, one of the most effective ways that apprentice climbers had of learning about what to expect during an expedition was to talk to those who had already been there.

There were few photographs of the most dangerous parts of any expedition. It was only by talking to climbers and explorers who had returned from these places that those setting off could learn about what to expect in the most remote regions and how best to prepare for what lay ahead. In this way, knowledge and wisdom were not only shared and passed on, but a whole body of information was built up. Also in this way, advancements in safety and equipment have been made as an entire library of knowledge was created through the mentoring chain.

The mentor-apprentice relationship can be either formal or informal. When we are learning skills across a range of areas, we can benefit from having mentors who offer

> **They light the way and provide tools we need**

support and further guidance. We may already know—or know of—these people, and can make direct contact with them and ask their advice. People are usually flattered to be asked and are generous in their response.

When we are actively engaged with our life journey, we are always looking for the best way to do things and to move forward. There is nothing better than learning from those who have gone before, particularly if they have left a legacy of excellence. Sometimes we want to make a clean sweep and do things differently, but it is foolhardy not to realise the intrinsic value of the knowledge and experience of those who have travelled the same path before us. Mentors light the way and give us the tools we need to make our own mark in the world.

When I started off in climbing, one of my most influential mentors was a man from Poland called Maciej Berbeka. He was my partner on two expeditions and taught me valuable lessons in high-altitude mountaineering. As an enthusiastic apprentice, I was always trying to prove that I was the fittest, best and most capable. He was taken by my enthusiasm but taught me that I needed to rein it in. Every day he would tell me to slow down, to pace myself, to look around and to observe my surroundings. Following Maciej's advice, I would arrive back at Base Camp after a full day's climbing with plenty of energy. In this way, I learned that success is infinitely more achievable when we move at the proper pace, neither under- nor over-extending ourself.

> **These lessons kept me alive**

I also learned to ensure that everything that I did within high-altitude mountaineering was thought out and meticulously planned, thereby minimising the need to take an uncalculated risk. These lessons have helped me remain alive in one of the highest-risk sports in the world where, to date, over 50 of my friends have lost their lives on the mountains. I learned these important lessons because of the interest that a fellow climber had in mentoring me in and teaching me what he knew. I, in turn, have become a mentor for other people, passing on the wise lessons—both in my adventure and business life—that I learned from Maciej about risk, planning and making common-sense decisions.

As mentors we should encourage apprentices in our areas of expertise. Sharing our knowledge and experience is a great way of re-examining it and learning anew. We can enjoy the thrill of passing on the baton to the next person and seeing how far they will take it.

- As a mentor you can encourage others' enthusiasm, passion and skill

- As a mentor you get a chance to express and revisit your passion

- As a mentor you receive great satisfaction in seeing apprentices take the skills and knowledge you have passed on to them to the next level

- As a mentor, you can facilitate the success of others

- As a mentor, you share the library of information and expertise in your head and heart that illuminates the way for the next generation

I have the power to:

- Be an effective team member
- Respect other team members
- Be an inspiring leader
- Learn the skills of self-leading
- Form effective partnerships
- Share my knowledge and expertise

WHAT'S NEXT?

Throughout our life we achieve many dreams and goals. Once a goal is reached, we set new goals and create new dreams. Our ambitions and desires evolve throughout our life and what was our 'Everest' challenge, once achieved, becomes a milestone on the journey to a new goal. When we have a goal, and a plan to achieve that goal, we have a sense of purpose and a focus. We see the road in front of us; we imagine our destination and we do all that we need to do to get there. Having goals and working to make them a reality gives us a sense—real or imagined—of control over our destiny. At the very least, we feel we are making an effort to actively engage in the process of creating the life that we want.

Achieving our goals is never easy and we may be tempted to give up during times of extreme frustration and difficulty. But we don't give up because, the longer we stay on the road, the more we become the kind of people who don't give up—either on ourself or our goal. We use our want as fuel to keep us going. And then, one day, we achieve our goal. That which we have worked towards becomes reality and we take a moment to celebrate.

The moment of achievement passes quickly even though the journey to it has taken months or even years. It may sound strange that, following the moment when we achieve **Use your want as a fuel to keep going** what we want, we might be thrown into confusion. We put so much of ourself into achieving our goals that, when we reach them, we can feel at a loss, not knowing exactly who we are or how to move forward now that we are no longer striving for this particular goal.

This can be a time of confusion and even despair. But it is natural after the high of reaching our goal that we experience the low of knowing a certain part of our journey is now over. We put so much of our time and energy into making our goal a reality that when it happens we can experience feelings that we didn't expect and that are unsettling.

This is why it is important to always have a 'What's next?' before we even reach our current goal. Part of our mind should already be

We are more than our achievements

thinking about the next thing we want to do, not because we should jump from one thing to the next without taking time for reflection, but because each goal is a journey with a destination and, once that destination is reached, we should know what our next one will be. By having a 'What's next?' we not only have the seed of a new goal waiting to be nurtured, we also recognise that while each goal is important, we will not be defined by its achievement. We are more and our life is more.

At 7.45am on 27 May 1995 my dream of standing on top of the world was about to become a reality. I was 38 years old and felt as if I was dying, but my will to live was stronger as I walked along that narrow ridge at 29,000 feet, a height at which jetliners cruise. It was a clear morning, with blue skies and -40 temperatures. I couldn't feel my fingers or toes and thought I was getting frostbite. I was gasping for air to survive in the Death Zone. Step by agonising step, I inched towards the summit of Mount Everest with my climbing partners, Mike Smith and James Allen. My dream was about to be realised.

When I stood on the summit of Everest for the first time, my exhaustion and fear that I was dying evaporated. I had never felt

We're standing on top of the world!

more alive as I stood with Mike and James on a patch of ground not much bigger than a kitchen table. I put my hand into my pocket and took out my country's national flag and placed it proudly on my ice axe. I raised my hands high in the air and shouted, 'Yes! We're standing on top of the world'. We had pushed ourself to the limit for 50 days, living in the confines of small tents strapped to the face of Everest, weathering storms and brutal winds and now we had arrived at its summit.

Very quickly, it was time to go. James, Mike and I hugged and, as we did, James whispered into my ear, *'What's next, Falvey?'*. I had already learned the lesson ten years earlier that we always need a 'What's next?' when my business—and only dream—had disappeared. Now I already had new plans. I smiled at James and said, 'I'm going to climb each of the highest mountains on each continent'.

Within two years I had achieved my goal of becoming the first Irish person to complete this challenge. In February 1997, while descending Mount Kosciuszko in Australia—the last of the Seven Summits—my climbing partner and friend, Con Moriarty, asked, 'What's next, Falvey?'. I already knew: I was going to lead the first Irish team to climb Everest from the south side and lead the first Irish female to its summit.

> The clock is ticking fast and my challenges are different

On 17 May 2004, I stood on the summit of Everest, for the second time, with Clare O'Leary who had just become the first Irish female to reach the summit of the world's highest mountain. I had achieved all three objectives that I had set myself and another dream was now a reality. Clare turned to me before leaving the summit and asked, 'What's next?'.

With Clare, I went on to complete the Seven Summits challenge to climb the highest point on each continent for a second time, becoming the first person in the world to do so by climbing Everest from both the north and south faces. As we stood on the summit of the final mountain, Clare again asked me, 'What's next?'.

Since then, my dreams of new adventures have taken me all around the world to the highest, coldest, loneliest and most remote regions on planet Earth. I have walked to the South Pole, across Greenland and to other Polar regions. I have trekked across deserts, jungles, glaciers and mountains. During my expeditions, I have had the privilege to work with over 30 different tribes of people. I've become fascinated by what drives us as humans to succeed, to dream, to dare and to do. Along the way I have become a motivational speaker, written books and produced films. I have also regained my passion for business and entrepreneurial work.

The years have flown by and I'm now 59 years old. I still have lots of exciting dreams and goals that I wish to achieve in my adventure, personal, spiritual and business life. The clock is ticking fast and my challenges are different but I know that I will want to achieve new goals until the day I die. Family and friends still ask me, 'What's next?'.

Right now my most important goals are to be the best grandfather

I can be to my grandchildren, and to help and inspire others to make the most of their lives by living their dreams and not just living in them.

We all need to have a 'What's next?'.

What's next for you?

I have the power to:

- *Explore the mindset I need to realise my dreams*

YOU HAVE THE POWER

PEAK PERFORMANCE & LIFETIME LEARNING PROGRAMMES INCLUDE:

- Seminars
- Workshops
- Team-building
- Personal development
- Challenge-based adventure holidays

PRESENTATIONS:

- You Have The Power
- The Mind Climb
- Operation Everest
- Beyond Endurance

PAT FALVEY works worldwide as an inspirational motivator and keynote speaker. Details of Peak Performance & Lifetime Learning Programmes, presentations, books, DVDs and adventure holidays are available at www.patfalvey.com

CONTACT DETAILS:

Address: The Mountain Lodge, Beaufort, Killarney, County Kerry, Ireland

Tel: 00353 (64) 6644181

Website: www.patfalvey.com

Email: info@patfalvey.com

Twitter: @patfalvey

Facebook: PatFalveyWorldwideAdventures/ PersonalDevelopment